People are talking about "hope" these days. It tells us of the need and speaks of their yearning. In this helpful book, Mac Brunson combines the teaching of the Scriptures and the heart of a pastor to point people to the Source of true and lasting hope.
—Ed Stetzer, President of LifeWay Research

I've known Mac since the nineties and have always wondered when he was going to write. Mac combines theological precision with ministerial experience and a pastor's heart. He understands worry not just from the Bible's perspective but also from working with lots and lots of worried people. I can't think of anyone better to write on this subject.
—Tommy Nelson, Senior Pastor, Denton Bible Church, Denton, Texas

Mac Brunson is a true shepherd. He has a keen eye for where Scripture connects to the lives of his people and applies it with sensitivity and precision. This book is loaded with solid exegesis and pastoral application, and I am glad to warmly recommend it.
—Dr. J.D. Greear, Pastor, The Summit Church, Durham, North Carolina

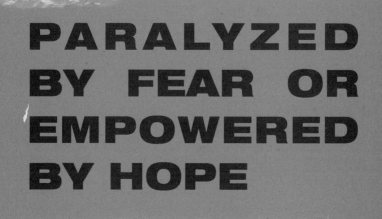

PARALYZED BY FEAR OR EMPOWERED BY HOPE

PARALYZED BY FEAR OR EMPOWERED BY HOPE

A Fresh Look at Psalm 23

Dr. Mac Brunson

NAVPRESS ⦿

NavPress is the publishing ministry of The Navigators, an international Christian organization and leader in personal spiritual development. NavPress is committed to helping people grow spiritually and enjoy lives of meaning and hope through personal and group resources that are biblically rooted, culturally relevant, and highly practical.

For a free catalog go to www.NavPress.com
or call 1.800.366.7788 in the United States or 1.800.839.4769 in Canada.

ISBN-13: 978-1-61521-563-8

Cover and Interior design by Liquid Lotus LLC

Some of the anecdotal illustrations in this book are true to life and are included with the permission of the persons involved. All other illustrations are composites of real situations, and any resemblance to people living or dead is coincidental.

Unless otherwise identified, all Scripture quotations in this publication are taken from the New American Standard Bible® (NASB), Copyright © 1960, 1962, 1963, 1968, 1971, 1972, 1973, 1975, 1977, 1995 by The Lockman Foundation. Used by permission.
Scripture quotations marked KJV are taken from the *King James Version* of the Bible.

Library of Congress Cataloging-in-Publication Data submitted.

Printed in the United States of America
1 2 3 4 5 6 7 8 / 13 12 11 10

Dedication

**To the girl who has dedicated her life
to making my life a dream come true...** *Debbie.*

Psalm 23

The Lord is my shepherd,
I shall not want.
He makes me lie down in green pastures;
He leads me beside quiet waters.
He restores my soul;
He guides me in the paths of righteousness
For His name's sake.

Even though I walk through the valley of the
shadow of death,
I fear no evil, for You are with me;
Your rod and Your staff, they comfort me.
You prepare a table before me in the presence
of my enemies;
You have anointed my head with oil;
My cup overflows.
Surely goodness and loving-kindness will
follow me all the days of my life,
And I will dwell in the house of the Lord forever.

Contents

Foreword

Following the conclusion of the Korean War, Major (Dr.) William E. Mayer studied one thousand Americans who had been detained in North Korean camps as prisoners of war. By conventional wartime standards, these camps were not particularly cruel or harsh. The American prisoners were provided with sufficient water, food, and shelter. And most were not subjected to physical torture or abuse. In fact, there were far fewer reports of physical abuse in the North Korean POW camps than in any other major military conflict throughout our nation's history. Yet despite the relatively good conditions, the overall death rate in the North Korean POW camps was an incredible thirty-eight percent—the highest POW death rate in United States military history.

Why did so many Americans perish in these camps? What Mayer discovered was that half of the American soldiers died *simply because they had given up*. According to Mayer, their captors employed a powerful psychological warfare that—while not denying any of their basic physical needs—put the soldiers "into a kind of emotional and psychological isolation, the likes of which we had never seen." Without anger to fuel their will to survive, the Americans just gave up. Mayer called this phenomenon *mirasmus*, meaning "a lack of resistance; a passivity." In other words, these soldiers died because they were hopeless.[1]

It would be impossible to estimate how many relationships, dreams, and futures have been lost due to hopelessness.

[1]Tom Rath, and Donald Clifton, *How Full is Your Bucket* (New York: Gallup Press, 2004), 17-19.

The Bible tells us that, "Hope deferred makes the heart sick," (Proverbs 13:12). Hopelessness produces a sickness that hinders, cripples, and most dangerous of all—it paralyzes.

As I write this foreword, I am visiting New York in order to lead a Bible study for those who work in the offices of the United Nations. I have been privileged to meet administrators, office personnel, and support staff for ambassadors from around the world. Many are from nations that are torn by strife and conflict, as well as some individuals whose countries are so poor they can barely afford to send representation to the United Nations. There are those whose governments are openly hostile toward Christianity, and many more who struggle with isolation and loneliness from being the only believer in their offices.

Yet there is a sense of hope among them that is amazing. Even in the darkest corners of this planet where people are oppressed by persecution, poverty, and war, those who are committed to the Lord Jesus Christ have a strength and resiliency that can only be explained by hope.

We can either choose to be paralyzed by fear, or we can be empowered by the hope that comes through a personal relationship with Jesus Christ. In the words of the great old hymn: *My hope is built on nothing less than Jesus' blood and righteousness.* That is the hope that is real; the foundation that produces life.

Acknowledgements

In this life, nothing of value is ever achieved alone. All along the way there are those who come to our aid, invest of themselves, or simply cheer us on when we need encouragement. I want to say a special thank you to my friend, Maurilio Amorim, and to all the folks at the A Group. At first a valued consultant, Maurilio has become one of my best friends, as well as a dear brother in Christ.

Mike Miller at NavPress is one of the "go to" guys in my life. He and his sweet wife, Pat, have been such an encouragement and comrades in arms. Thank you for your friendship and for the times you have stood with me, for me, and behind me.

I would also like to thank my son, Trey, for handling so many of the details that are necessary in completing a project of this magnitude that I would simply overlook and forget about. Thanks son.

And finally, to the congregation at First Baptist Church Jacksonville, which is made up of the choicest people in all the earth. Every week I have the highest privilege of preaching to one of the greatest congregations in all of Christendom. You are so supportive and exemplify the fruit of the Spirit in a way that shines across the city and around the world. Debbie and I dearly love our large, extended family at FBC JAX.

Chapter 1

WORRY –
THE FAMILIAR FACE
OF FEAR

The LORD is my shepherd, I shall not want
—Psalm 23:1

Sherlock Holmes, Sir Arthur Conan Doyle's famous fictional detective, is legendary for his astute observations. One of his more memorable quotes appears in the short story *A Scandal in Bohemia*, when Holmes uncovers an important truth for his faithful sidekick, Dr. Watson.

"You see, but you do not observe. The distinction is clear. For example you have frequently seen the steps which lead up from the hall to this room."

Watson responds: "Frequently."

Holmes then asks: "How often?"

Watson: "Well, some hundreds of times."

Holmes: "Then how many are there?"

Watson: "How many? I don't know."

Holmes: "Quite so! You have not observed. And yet you have seen. That is just my point. I know that there are seventeen steps, because I have both seen and observed."

Have you ever felt like Dr. Watson must have in that moment? Knowing that the answer is right in front of you, but you can't quite put your finger on it? That something is perfectly obvious to everyone else, but somehow you've missed it? As the saying goes, "The devil is in the details."

There is one thing that we all have seen at one time or another—fear. What many people do not realize is that fear takes many forms, among them anxiety, stress, panic, and obsession. But perhaps the most common face of fear is *worry*. We have all worried about a situation or circumstance we just knew would be disastrous; something we were certain would be completely devastating, only to see it eventually work out. We have *seen* this happen time and again in our own lives, only, as Sherlock Holmes would be quick to point out, we have not *observed*. We have not observed God's hand at work, so we've missed the most important detail in the situation. Because of that, when the next problem comes along we find ourselves running scared and are consumed with worry all over again.

Fortunately, God's Word gives us a wealth of insight into the face of fear that we know as worry. In fact, David addresses the issue in one of the most familiar and beloved passages in all of Scripture: Psalm 23. Now many theologians have debated over exactly when David wrote this psalm. Some say that he wrote it at the height of his reign as King of Israel. Others say he wrote it as an old man looking back over his life. But I suspect he wrote it when he was just a boy, watching over his father's sheep.

When God sent Samuel to the village of Bethlehem and the house of Jesse to anoint the next king of Israel, the Lord told him, "I'm going to show you the one that I have chosen to be King." Well, when Jesse paraded out his seven big, strong, and strapping sons, Samuel was pretty impressed. But as Samuel went down the line from the first to the last, he knew none of them were God's man. So he looked at Jesse and said, "Do you have one more?" And Jesse answered, "Yes, the youngest is out watching the sheep." Such an important occasion and it never occurred to them to call David in from the field!

David probably felt overlooked and neglected at times. Perhaps he was alone in the field one evening, thinking about all the things he had done for those sheep during the course of the day. "*I have watched over them, I have protected them, and I have defended them. I've walked in front of them, behind them, and in the midst of them. I have nursed those that were sick, I have chased after some that went astray, and I have led them to the places where they needed to go, keeping them away from danger. And finally, I've brought them safely home, back to the sheepfold."*

I can just imagine David sitting there thinking, *"Now this is what I have done as a shepherd for these sheep, but who does this for me? Who watches over me, guides me, comforts me, protects me, leads me, directs me...* who shepherds the shepherd?" And then David realized, "The Lord is my Shepherd. *Having done all of these things for the sheep as their shepherd, now I understand the Lord also does all of these things for me. And if God does all of this for me, why do I worry about the things of life?"*

David didn't just see a bunch of smelly sheep in the field—he observed something important about the nature of God. And the more you know and understand about God, the less fear will consume your life.

Four Truths About Worry

Now, there are four important characteristics to keep in mind about worry. Number one, *worry is unhelpful*. It never accomplishes anything. Worry is like sitting with your car in park while you press your foot on the gas. Do you remember back in your younger days, when you'd stop at a red light and a good-looking girl would pull up beside you? The clutch was in, and you would sit there revving that engine, doing anything you could to get her attention. And that's what worry is like. It creates a lot of noise,

fumes, and smoke, but it accomplishes absolutely nothing. You're stuck in park, with the engine running, and you're going nowhere.

Worry is also *unreasonable*. Let's be honest—worrying really is a useless exercise. As Spock, a fictional character in the Star Trek franchise, would say, "it is not logical." If you are worried about something you are powerless to change, why are you worried about it? There is nothing you can do. You cannot change it. If you are struggling with a situation you can change—then do what needs to be done. But if it is an unchangeable or uncontrollable thing, why do you worry? What is the point?

The third characteristic of worry is that it is *unhealthy*. Your body was not designed to worry. Charles Mayo, co-founder of the Mayo Clinic, studied what happens to the body when people worry. As a result of his work, he made the observation that worry adversely affects the circulatory system, the heart, the glands, and the entire nervous system. In the medical journal *American Mercury*, Mayo wrote that he never knew of anyone that died of overwork, but that he knew many who died of worry. You cannot worry yourself into a longer or better life, but you absolutely can worry yourself to death.

Finally, *worry is unnatural*. Many people use the expression "natural born worrier." Well, that is not accurate, we are not born pre-disposed to worry—it is a learned behavior. In fact, it requires a great deal of practice to become good at it. But what David is saying in this first verse of Psalm 23 is that you and I can face the imminent, the inevitable, and the unknown without the worry that is produced by fear and brings distress. You may be wondering, "*How do I do that?*" You can handle anything that comes if you know God. That's what David is really saying. "The Lord is my Shepherd. I know God. And that does something to eliminate this whole process of worry in my life." Worry is an unnatural behavior for those who know God.

Past, Present, and Future

David begins Psalm 23 with two simple, yet profound words: "THE LORD." Now, some translations of the Bible capitalize "Lord" to indicate that this is the noun *Jehovah*, which is the transliteration of the name *Yahweh*. That single noun combines all three tenses of the Hebrew verb "to be." *Jeh*, is He will be; *Ov*, is simply being, in the present tense; *Ah*, is past tense. That one word sums up the fact that God is eternal—He is the God who was, who is, and who will be.

So when David says "The LORD," he is essentially saying, "This is the God who addresses my past. This is the God who is present in the here and now. And this is the God who is God of the future and all of eternity." That is exactly what the writer of the book of Hebrews tells us, "Jesus Christ is the same yesterday and today and forever," (Hebrews 13:8).

David is telling us that as believers, it is unnecessary for us to worry about the past. God is Lord of the past. It's unnecessary to worry about the present. He is God of the present.

It is unnecessary to worry about the future. He is the God who is already there and holds it all in His hands.

Right now you may be thinking, *"That's easier said than done! You don't know all of the problems I'm facing in my life right now."* It's true—so many of us today are worried about things we used to take for granted. It's funny how times can change us. We used to worry about having extravagant things, but now we have to focus on the basics. We worry about putting food on the table. About keeping a roof over our family's heads. Wondering how we are going to put our children through school.

But you can't justify or rationalize worrying by pointing to your problems—the effect on your life is too devastating. The word *worry* comes from an old English word that means to "choke or strangle." And that is exactly what worry does. It will suffocate you, strangle your joy, and choke the life right out of you.

Listen to what Jesus said in Matthew 6:25: "For this reason I say to you, do not be worried about your life, as to what you will eat or what you will drink; nor for your body, as to what you will put on."

Jesus is speaking directly to all of those basic needs that we can spend so much time worrying about. And to put it simply, Jesus said, "Stop it." The verb tense He uses here literally means to stop whatever worrying is already in process and don't start worrying about anything else. Later on in verse 34, Jesus says, "So do not worry about tomorrow." That is the future imperative. Jesus is saying that if you are not worried now, don't start. Don't let it become a habit. Don't let this act of fear become something in your life that grips you day after day. Why? Because He is God. He is in charge. If you call Him Lord, then He will take care of you.

The Work of the Shepherd

Let's look again at the words that David wrote: "The Lord is my shepherd." David begins with the name of *Jehovah*, and then he claims God as his own personal shepherd. He doesn't say, "He is *a* shepherd" or "He is *the* Shepherd." He says, "He is *my* Shepherd." He claims possession and ownership by God. If you are a believer, then God is *your* shepherd also.

Now shepherds were always a despised people. Keeping sheep was not considered to be a noble, honorable, or desired profession. David was the youngest of eight boys and he was stuck with the job of tending the sheep. Then why does God compare Himself to a shepherd? Remember, David is thinking about his own work with the sheep and how God cares for him in the same way.

David knew that there are four critical things that a shepherd does for the sheep. The first is he **provides**. Shepherds must provide food, water, and all the other necessities of life. Sheep cannot provide anything for themselves. They are incredibly helpless animals. If a flock of sheep were left alone in a pasture, they would eat the grass clean down to the dirt and destroy the land. They would turn it into a desert. So if the shepherd does not regularly guide them to new fields, sheep would just sit there and starve to death because there's no grass left. They are not very intelligent animals.

Second, the shepherd **protects**. We know that David himself fought off a lion and, on another occasion, a bear that had come after the flock. Sheep have no natural defense; they have no way to protect themselves. Wouldn't it be something if the evening news carried a report about some sheep taking off one night to hunt wolves, attacking them, and eating them? It just doesn't happen because sheep are not aggressive animals. They don't have the capability to defend themselves against predators. They must have a shepherd to protect them.

Next, the shepherd **guides**. Sheep have no sense of direction and very poor eyesight. If they see something moving in front of them, they'll follow it, even if that takes them right off a cliff. Sheep don't have the ability to find their way back home like dogs or other animals with directional abilities. Sheep need to be guided. They are a lot like people—many times we follow whatever is put in front of us, even if it leads to certain destruction.

And finally, a shepherd **directs**. The shepherd is responsible for directing the sheep when their behavior leads toward danger. That's what a shepherd does for the sheep and what God does for us. He directs us away from that which is harmful, He directs us through the valley of the shadow of death, He directs us back home again.

So a shepherd does these four things for the sheep: provides, protects, guides, and directs. That is exactly what God does for us. Isaiah 40:11 says, "Like a shepherd He will tend His flock, in His arm He will gather the lambs and carry them in His bosom." Now, if God promises to do all of that for us, then what is left for us to worry about?

Real Sheep Don't Worry

Every aspect of this promise holds true in your life if you can say the Lord is your shepherd. Remember, David said "the LORD is *my* shepherd." In reality, the Lord is not everyone's shepherd. He is shepherd to those who know Him as Lord. He cannot be *your* shepherd unless He is your Lord.

What does it mean for Him to be Lord? It means we recognize that He is in charge of our lives. Jesus said "I am the good shepherd, and I know My own and My own know Me," (John 10:14). If you are a Christian, then Jesus says, "I know you and you know Me." He later goes on to say, "My sheep hear My voice, and I know them, and they follow Me; and I give eternal life to them, and they will never perish; and no one will snatch them out of My hand. My Father, who has given them to Me, is greater than all; and no one is able to snatch them out of the Father's hand. I and the Father are one," (John 10:27-30).

So the Lord says that His sheep know Him, listen to Him, and follow Him. Do you know Him? Do you hear His voice and follow Him? That is what it means for Jesus to be Lord. And He makes it very clear that absolutely nothing can snatch you out of the Father's hands. So why do you worry?

Worry and faith are incompatible. The very nature of worry makes it uncharacteristic of the Christian life and it will destroy your faith. Why? Because, ultimately worry is sin. You see, worry is really a control issue. Worry is an attempt to control the uncontrollable. Worry is assuming responsibilities that you were never meant to have. Any time you try to control what is out of your control you are going to worry. We think, *"I have to get control of this situation... this job... this marriage ... this teenager, if it's the last thing I do."* But the real question we should be asking ourselves is, *"Who is in control here?"* Only God is really in control of everything. If you are in a state of fearful worry, can you truthfully say, "The LORD is my shepherd?"

Listen, the Lord will not force Himself on you. You have free will, the option of whether or not you will surrender control of your life to Him. Now if you are in control, that means He is not. If you are in control of your life and not God, then you really do have a reason to be worried.

Nothing but Vapor and Smoke

Now let me ask a question of you: Based on your past experiences and your present situation, don't you think God will be able to take care of your tomorrows? You may be going through a tough time, but I'm confident that you have not lacked something that you really needed. You may have lacked something that you *wanted*, but the very fact that you have survived to this point means God has provided for you.

Moses said this very thing to the Hebrew children after they had wandered for forty years in the wilderness: "For the LORD your God has blessed you in all that you have done; He has known your wanderings through this great wilderness. These forty years the LORD your God has been with you; you have not lacked a thing," (Deuteronomy 2:7).

You have not gone through one single thing in your life that God doesn't know about. Have you declared bankruptcy? God knows that. Did you go through a divorce? God was right there. Have you suffered a serious illness? Lost your job? Lost a loved one? God has not left your side. He is the Shepherd of your life if you know Him as Lord and Savior. Listen again to what He says, "He has known your wanderings." He knows what you are going through in this great wilderness.

Now if we look at the rest of this remarkable verse, Psalm 23:1 goes on to say, "The LORD is my shepherd, *I shall not want*." David is looking to the future and affirms that he is connected to the source that is all-sufficient and inexhaustible. In other words, he is not going to worry about all of those things that he might need, all of the things that can go wrong, all of the things in life that can fall apart. He is telling us that based on past and present experiences we can trust God for the future.

A University of Michigan study discovered some interesting facts about fear and worry:

- 60% of what you worry about is unwarranted.
- 20% of what you worry about is already past; it is over and done with.

- 10% are issues so petty that it is foolish to worry about them.
- 4% to 5% are justifiable concerns, but there is nothing you can do about them; they are out of your hands.
- Only 2% of what we fear and worry about is legitimate.

You see, so much of what we worry about is not real. Worry exacerbates; it exaggerates the situation and creates a monster that stands larger than life. Do you remember the old Godzilla movies where the monster towered over skyscrapers and stomped flat everything in its path? That is what worry does in your life. It becomes bigger than everything else, even God. That is the sin of worry—it replaces God in your life.

One morning not long ago, I was driving into town and it was so foggy I couldn't see a thing. I couldn't see the bridge I crossed over; I couldn't see downtown, the river, or anything else. I could barely see a couple of feet in front of my car. As I drove through that mess I remembered something that I had once read about fog.

Did you know that if you take a dense fog that is one hundred feet deep and covers seven square city blocks and condense it, you would get less than one single eight-ounce glass of water? When a single cup of water is vaporized, it transforms into a dense, blinding fog that covers seven city blocks. That's amazing!

And that is what we do with worry. We allow something in our life—whatever it may be—that amounts to almost nothing, to become a blinding, all-encompassing vapor that hinders our faith. We sit in park, blowing smoke from our exhaust that keeps us from experiencing the Christian life God wants us to have.

But let me tell you, there is freedom from worry. Condense all of those problems you carry right now back down to their real size and place them in the hands of the Lord. Allow God, your Shepherd, to lead and guide you, and you too will be able to declare, "*The LORD is my Shepherd, I shall not want.*"

Chapter 2

RESTLESSNESS

He makes me lie down in green pastures;
He leads me beside quiet waters.

—Psalm 23:2

Several years ago *Ring* magazine, the well-known publication of the boxing world, published a story about one of the most unusual events in boxing history. Now boxing has always interested me because my father fought Golden Gloves. And this particular article was about a Golden Gloves Championship fight that literally was over before it even began.

We've all seen athletes on television getting pumped up to compete against their opponents. Some "trash talk" and boast of their skills, others may gesture wildly, pound their chest, or bounce around in an attempt to get their adrenaline pumping. But on this particular occasion, the contender was a little too good at his warm-up routine. He was so intent on psyching himself into a fighting mood that he punched himself in the face. The first self-inflicted blow cracked his jaw. The second broke his nose and rendered him unconscious. The unfortunate boxer was carried away on a stretcher before his opponent ever stepped into the ring.

There is an important lesson to be learned from this true story. Many times it is not what the other guy does that will knock you out—it is often what you do to yourself that can inflict the greatest damage. And that is true for all of us. So often our fears become self-fulfilling prophecies. Job said, "For what I fear comes upon me, and what I dread befalls me," (Job 3:25). We all have the capability of sabotaging our own lives if we allow our fears to determine our destiny. Fear can lead to self-inflicted blows that we may never be able to recover from.

A Restless Generation

One of the primary ways we sabotage our own lives is by refusing to follow the leadership of the Lord. We know that worry comes from the fear of not being in control. But another characteristic of fear is *restlessness*. Restlessness occurs when we start thinking to ourselves, "*I am not in charge; I am not leading.*" It is an authority issue. Who is going to be in charge?

Restlessness is perhaps the best word I know to sum up our generation. If there is one defining characteristic of our western culture, it is that we are a nation of bored, restless people who want to be in control of every aspect of our lives. And it is no different in the church.

John Zogby, the president and CEO of Zogby International, has written a book entitled, *The Way We Will Be*. Zogby is a well-known American pollster who has conducted polls and focus groups around the world, although he has gained the most publicity for his polls of United States Presidential elections. Using all of the data and information he has gathered, Zogby offers a fascinating glimpse at what our culture might be like fifteen or twenty years in the future.

In one chapter Zogby talks about the "new" American dream and looks at different subsets of our nation. One of those groups he calls the "Secular Spiritualists"—people who say that the answers to America's problems are spiritual, yet they live like the rest of secular society. *Secular Spiritualists*. What a contradiction in terms! That title fascinates me because it seems to be what so many Christians have settled for. We claim spirituality but really we are secular to the core. We are secular in our thinking and in our behavior. If someone asks, "How do we solve the world's problems?" we would say, *"Well, the world needs Jesus ... and faith in God. We believe in the power of prayer and the life and ministry of the church."* And yet, the way we live our daily lives is no different from our secular neighbors.

Newsweek asked the following question of evangelical Christian teens: "Can a good person who does not share your religious beliefs attain salvation or go to heaven?" Sixty-eight percent said "**yes**." Think about that for a moment... two-thirds of teenagers raised in the church believe that there is no significant difference between their own faith and other religions.

Now if Christianity was merely a system of beliefs, they might have a point. If Christianity were simply based on ethical teachings or theological concepts then it would just be one religion among many. Then we could debate which one was superior.

Most religions are based on philosophical propositions or theological ideologies. Remove the teacher or the guru, and the religion still remains. That is not the case with Christianity— it is based on the life, character, and identity of one person: Jesus Christ.

Jesus did not come to earth to teach Christianity, He **is** Christianity. Remove Jesus from the equation and Christianity collapses. Christianity is not about Jesus coming to teach bad people how to be better. It is about Christ coming to earth to raise dead people to new life through a relationship with Him.[1]

The problem is we want to remove from our daily lives the inconvenient realities of following Jesus. We don't have a truly biblical, Christian worldview. In other words—what we *believe* and what we *do* are from two separate worlds. Why has this happened? **Because we want to be in control**. That's the bottom line.

We think to ourselves, "*I have to be in charge of my life, I absolutely cannot let someone else be in charge. I can't even let the Lord be in charge of my life because I've got to handle these things, I've got to be responsible, I've got to make it*

[1] Josh McDowell, *The Last Christian Generation* (Holiday, Florida: Green Key Books, 2006), 35-37.

happen." We tell ourselves that if we put our lives in God's hands that He is going to put more on us than we can manage.

But that's not really the issue. God doesn't give us more than we can handle. Jesus said, "For My yoke is easy and My burden is light," (Matthew 11:30). The truth is that we know God is going to ask us to give up some things that we don't want to let go of. He is going to restrict some areas in our lives that are outside His will. That's the problem. We know He will call the shots and we don't want to submit to His authority. And that has left us a restless people.

Who Is in Charge?

Who should be in charge of your life? The answer to restlessness lies in trusting the Shepherd to lead. If we look closely, we see that David talks about that very thing in Psalm 23:2. He writes, "He makes me lie down in green pastures; He leads me beside quiet waters." It always amazes me how much the Word of God can convey in just a few words. "He makes me... He leads me..." Who is in charge here?

"He *makes*." We don't want anybody *making* us do anything. But that speaks of God acting on His authority. Then, "He *leads*." Once again, that goes against the grain. *That's not what I want. I don't want Him leading. I want to be in charge. I want my way.* After all, that is human nature.

Have you ever tried to "make" a two-year-old do something he doesn't want to do? One afternoon I was watching my two grandsons while my wife and daughter went out to run some errands. Fortunately, the baby was sleeping, and I settled on the couch with the two-year-old to watch Bonanza. *No sweat*, I thought, *I can introduce him to some good television and we'll have a great time while the baby sleeps. What could possibly go wrong?*

Well, if you have ever been around young children, I'm sure you know that the answer to that question is **anything**! Sure enough, the next moment he fell over and hit his head on the end table. Naturally, he started screaming and I thought, "*Please, please don't wake the baby up; whatever you do, don't wake the baby up.*" So I grabbed him and ran to the refrigerator, pulled out an ice pack and put it on his head. Then I laid him down; all the while he was wailing and throwing a fit.

"Sshhh, sshhh... it's okay... let's just lie down... calm down, everything will be alright," I said to him. And what did he do? He popped right back up. Just like a little jack-in-the-box. He sat up, stared at me, and screamed. I laid him back down again, but he kept screaming and sitting up over and over—he was having none of it.

Isn't that how we are with God? Jesus Christ comes to us as the great Shepherd, and He tries in the midst of our hurt to get us to lie down and rest in His supply. And what do we keep doing? We keep popping back up and hollering, "I'm hurt! I'm hurt! I'm hurt!"

We are restless. We don't have enough time. No matter how exhausted, tired, or weary we are, fear makes us believe that everything will fall apart if we don't keep after it. No one can do it but us. No one can handle it but us. We are just like little children who will not lie down to rest.

Problems that Trouble the Flock

David said, "He makes me lie down," because as a shepherd, he knew that sheep are not particularly cooperative. And we are the same way. We want to be in charge of our lives instead of letting God take control. We don't recognize that He has brought us to a place where we can relax and trust Him to meet all of our needs.

There was a wonderful devotional book written by Phillip Keller many years ago, called *A Shepherd Looks at the Good Shepherd*. And according to Keller, a shepherd himself, it is almost impossible to get sheep to lie down unless four specific problems are addressed.

The first problem is no surprise: *fear*. Fear has to be eliminated. Now sheep are very fitful, timid animals. Because they have no natural defenses, even the smallest movement creates a distraction for them and they will react in fear. Sheep will not rest as long as they see or hear things moving, unless the shepherd comes and stands in the midst of them. Only then will they settle down.

Really, people are the same way. How many young children go to bed but can't sleep because they are afraid of "monsters" under their beds or in the closet? The slightest sound or shadow can send them into a state of panic. And then, they often need the presence and intervention of their parents to bring comfort and assurance.

As adults, we really are no different. A perfect example happened when Jesus was in a boat with His disciples on the Sea of Galilee. "And there arose a fierce gale of wind, and the waves were breaking over the boat so much that the boat was already filling up. Jesus Himself was in the stern, asleep on the cushion; and they woke Him and said to Him, 'Teacher, do You not care that we are perishing?' And He got up and rebuked the wind and said to the sea, 'Hush, be still.' And the wind died down and it became perfectly calm. And He said to them, 'Why are you afraid? How is it that you have no faith?'" (Mark 4:37-40).

We are fearful of so many things in life. Every little storm gets us all worked up. But if we could see that Jesus Christ is right here in our midst and He is in charge, we would find peace and rest.

The second problem that must be dealt with is **friction**. Sheep are very social creatures and if there is any kind of friction in the flock, they will not rest. Phillip Keller describes how sometimes the old ewes will charge the lambs. If a lamb is in a spot where a ewe wants to rest, graze, or lie down, that cranky ewe will stiffen her legs, lower her head, and run straight at the lamb, butting it out of the way. And when that's going on, the sheep will not rest.

Does that sound a little familiar? *Time* magazine once published an article entitled *Twentieth Century Blues: Stress, Anxiety, and Depression*. The article stated that humans have a fundamental need to connect with other people and the reason that our modern-day culture is so stressed out is because we have failed in so many of our relationships. What does that reveal about us?

We experience so much stress in life, and it is almost always relational. If we don't have conflict with someone at home, then inevitably it will be someone at the office or at church; in the neighborhood or at school. Why is that? We fear not being in control. We want to control every aspect of our lives. So we get offended and then stay angry; usually it is much ado about nothing, but we act like it is everything. What's the point of getting so worked up? Friction will bring you nothing but restlessness.

The next problem that can trouble the flock is **frustration**. Sheep will not rest as long as there is something frustrating them. Now, you may be wondering to yourself, "*What could possibly frustrate a sheep?*" It's not a very pleasant thing to think about, but a significant cause of frustration for sheep is parasites. They get inside their ears and noses and cause irritation and infection. It's like a never-ending itch that they can't scratch. That is one reason why a shepherd always carries a cruse of oil. In the late afternoon when the sheep lie down for the evening, the shepherd will take the oil and rub it into their ears and noses to cleanse and protect their skin.

Like the sheep, we can also become frustrated by the small irritations of our daily lives. The obnoxious buzz of an alarm clock is enough to start our day off on the wrong foot. Struggles with the computer; an extra-long wait in line for our morning coffee; the snarl of the daily commute; trying to navigate an automated phone system. All of these modern-day "conveniences" that were designed to make our lives better, simpler, easier, and faster, many times can create a continual state of aggravation, which leaves us feeling frustrated and restless.

Finally, sheep need *food*. If that shepherd has not led the sheep into green pastures to get their fill for the day, they will not lie down and rest. They will not be content until they have fully satisfied their hunger.

I honestly think that one of the major issues Christians struggle with today is spiritual emptiness. It is possible to go to church regularly, hear the Word, have relationships with other believers, listen to the sermon, and still starve spiritually. In fact, it happens over and over again. The writer of Hebrews talks about this very thing: "For everyone who partakes *only* of milk is not accustomed to the word of righteousness, for he is an infant. But solid food is for the mature, who because of practice have their senses trained to discern good and evil," (Hebrews 5:13-14).

The original word used here for "not accustomed" does not mean unfamiliar or ignorant, it means unskilled or untried. The reason so many people in our churches today are spiritually hungry is that when they hear the Word of God, they don't know what to do with it. They have not practiced or developed any skill at applying the Word to their daily lives. They hear a sermon but walk out of church as empty as they were when they walked in. No wonder we are restless—our spiritual bellies are growling and we are desperately looking for something to satisfy our hunger.

Jesus said, "I am the bread of life; he who comes to Me will not hunger, and he who believes in Me will never thirst," (John 6:35). Only the Shepherd can truly satisfy our needs.

Waters of Rest

In the second half of Psalm 23:2, David writes "He leads me beside quiet waters." Now the King James version says, "... beside still waters." Through the years I have heard some people interpret that to mean these were waters that did not flow or move. Others have suggested that sheep will not drink from running water. Well, let me tell you, if sheep are thirsty enough, they will drink from almost anything. That is not what it means. The Hebrew translation of this phrase literally means, "... beside the *waters of rest*." In other words, He leads me beside waters that are restful.

One other important thing to notice here is that David uses the plural form of "water." When you are thirsty, you might ask, "Can you please bring me a glass of water?" Or on a hot summer day you might suggest, "Let's go for a swim in the water." You wouldn't use the plural form, "waters," in those situations. So why is it used here? David is saying that the Shepherd will lead you repeatedly—over and over again—to places where water is restful. He does not provide for you just one time; every single time you allow the Lord to lead you, He will guide you beside waters of rest, to the place where your needs are met.

Throughout scripture God reassures His people that He will care for them and provide for all their needs—including rest. If you look back to the time when God brought the Hebrews up and out of Egypt, Moses told them that God would lead them not only to the promised land that flowed with milk and honey, but also to a place of rest, (see Deuteronomy 12:8-10).

Later in the book of Ezekiel, the Lord says:

> *"Thus says the LORD God, 'Behold, I Myself will search for My sheep and seek them out. As a shepherd cares for his herd in the day when he is among his scattered sheep, so I will care for My sheep and will deliver them from all the places to which they were scattered on a cloudy and gloomy day.*
>
> *"I will bring them out from the peoples and gather them from the countries and bring them to their own land; and I will feed them on the mountains of Israel, by the streams, and in all the inhabited places of the land.*
>
> *"I will feed them in a good pasture, and their grazing ground will be on the mountain heights of Israel. There they will lie down on good grazing ground and feed in rich pasture on the mountains of Israel.*
>
> *I will feed My flock and* **I will lead them to rest**, *' declares the LORD God."*
>
> —Ezekiel 34:11-15

Now here is the problem—instead of trusting our Shepherd's direction, we are constantly detouring, deviating, and departing from His leadership. That is why so many of us are worn out and exhausted. When we refuse to follow the Lord, we miss the blessing that He has for us. I have had so many believers come and say to me, "How in the world did I ever get in this situation?" Well, the answer is usually pretty simple—it's because *we've* been in charge of our own lives. We take our own detour and veer farther and farther off course. As a result we get lost and end up restless, weary, and fatigued.

Recovery from Restlessness

There are four different kinds of fatigue that we can experience. The first is *physical* fatigue, and, usually, we can take a vacation, or rest for a day or two and our bodies will recover. The next two are closely connected—*mental* and *emotional* fatigue. And generally it will take more than just a day or two to recover from either. Now, much like worry, mental and emotional fatigue can have a negative impact on your physical body as well. In fact, research shows that your physical endurance is affected by your mental and emotional wellness.

The fourth kind is *spiritual* fatigue and that comes from going our own way; from letting sin gain a foothold in our lives. Generally, if you are spiritually fatigued, you may feel hopeless and that you can't get past whatever struggle you are facing. You may think, "*I can't resist this temptation ... I'm just trapped*

*by this sin and I can't get out of it. I can't make good decisions.
I know what the Bible says, but that won't work for me."* If that
sounds familiar to you, then it is safe to say that Jesus Christ is
not in charge of your life. You are spiritually fatigued and you
are restless.

How do we recover from restlessness? Remember, David
said that if we allow the Lord to be our Shepherd, He will **make**
us lie down in green pastures. He does all the work. He will take
you to the place where all of your needs will be provided for, and
every day He will lead you beside waters that are restful. All you
have to do is follow His cue. You just let the Lord set the pace for
your life.

How do we do that? Well, we have to be watchful, attentive, and obedient to His lead. Not long ago I went to my very
first NASCAR race—the Daytona 500. It was pretty interesting
to see all of the cars, check out the pits, and learn about the
logistics of racing. One thing that really fascinated me was the
pace car. This particular one was a 2010 Chevy Camaro, with
426 hp and a 6.2l V8 engine. The interesting thing about this
pace car was that it had a specially designed strobe light
system so that every racecar—even those in the back—could
see it clearly no matter where it was located on the track.

The pace car does just that—it sets the pace, but not
just at the beginning of the race. If there is an emergency, an accident, or dangerous conditions on the track, the pace car will
immediately pull out in front of the leading racecar and will flash
its lights to slow everyone down until the emergency is over and
it is safe to proceed.

Whenever that car came out, all of a sudden every single racecar would slow down and move in behind it. It was amazing to see all of those cars line up like a bunch of baby ducks waddling after their mama. Some of the greatest names in racing were there that day, and those cars—worth hundreds of thousands of dollars—could have outrun that Camaro without trying. Yet every one of them submitted to the direction and guidance of the pace car.

If these daring and thrill-seeking drivers have enough sense to follow a pace car, why is it that we as Christians can't seem to follow the Good Shepherd? Is He not watching out for us? Does He not already know what troubles and challenges we face? Has He not promised to care for our every need?

The question is this: Who is setting the pace for your life? Will you submit to the Great Shepherd's authority and let Him lead you? Will you let Him set the pace and lead you to a place of rest?

Chapter 3

THE FEAR
OF NO RETURN

He restores my soul…

—Psalm 23:3a

Robert Robinson was like a lot of teenagers—a bit reckless, always looking for a little adventure, and not overly concerned about the future. And, given the opportunity, he was more than willing to indulge in some gambling and drinking with his buddies.

Now, his life had been difficult—his father had died when he was a child and his mother had struggled to raise him on her own with very little money. But he worked to help make ends meet and was studious and intelligent. One Sunday evening when he was sixteen, he was out with a bunch of friends when they decided it would be great fun to torment a half-drunk psychic who could "read their fortunes."

What seemed like harmless fun became a real turning point in Robert's life. The psychic told him that he "would live to see his children and grandchildren." This was unsettling to Robert, perhaps because his own father had died at such a young age. But he became determined to improve his situation in life through his education.

Then, not long after the episode with the psychic, he had a "divine appointment" with a traveling evangelist who caused Robert to consider not only where his choices were leading him in life, but also what consequences lay ahead for his soul. A little more than three years later, at the age of twenty, he surrendered his life to Christ and went into the ministry.

Now Robert was a gifted minister and writer and people quickly took notice of his exceptional abilities. He was just twenty-five years of age when a famous Baptist church in Cambridge called him to become its pastor. His fame spread rapidly and his future seemed exceedingly bright. But at the height of his preaching ministry he fell into immorality, and his star faded as quickly as it had appeared.

Years later Robert was traveling when he found himself seated next to a lady who was intently reading a book. At one point she asked Robert if he would read a passage and explain to her what the writer was saying. Robert picked up the book and, to his surprise, he read these words:

Come, Thou Fount of every blessing,
Tune my heart to sing Thy grace;
Streams of mercy, never ceasing,
Call for songs of loudest praise.
Teach me some melodious sonnet,
Sung by flaming tongues above.
Praise his Name, I'm fixed upon it,
Name of Thy redeeming love.

Sorrowing I shall be in spirit,
Till released from flesh and sin,
Yet from what I do inherit,
Here Thy praises I'll begin;
Here I raise my Ebenezer;
Here by Thy great help I've come;
And I hope, by Thy good pleasure,
Safely to arrive at home.

Jesus sought me when a stranger,
Wandering from the fold of God;
He, to rescue me from danger,
Interposed His precious blood;
How His kindness yet pursues me
Mortal tongue can never tell,

Clothed in flesh, till death shall loose me
I cannot proclaim it well.

O to grace how great a debtor
Daily I'm constrained to be!
Let Thy goodness, like a fetter,
Bind my wandering heart to Thee.
Prone to wander, Lord, I feel it,
Prone to leave the God I love;
Here's my heart, O take and seal it,
Seal it for Thy courts above.

O that day when freed from sinning,
I shall see Thy lovely face;
Clothed then in blood washed linen
How I'll sing Thy sovereign grace;
Come, my Lord, no longer tarry,
Take my ransomed soul away;
Send thine angels now to carry
Me to realms of endless day.

I'm sure the poor woman was quite confused when Robert abruptly handed the book back, looked away, and tried to change the subject. But for some reason she felt the need to press him for a response. *What did the writer mean? What was he talking about? Could he help her understand?* Finally, Robert revealed that he himself had written those very words!

He said, "Madam, I am the poor unhappy man who wrote that hymn many years ago, and I would give a thousand worlds, if I had them, to enjoy the feelings I had then."

A life that held so much promise—that had been undeniably saved and called by God—ended in bitterness, despair, and disillusionment. He longed for the joy and peace he had known when he was new in Christ. But like so many believers today, he had reached a point in his life where he had lost all hope. He was so burdened by sin, brokenness, and hurt that he was afraid to turn to God. He was convinced that he had reached the point of no return. What Robert Robinson needed more than anything else was for God to restore his soul.

Turn Around

One of the great fears that we face in life is that fear of no return—and it can paralyze us just like it did Robert Robinson. The truth is, life is hard. We all make mistakes. We all sin. We get beat up and hurt, and go through periods where it seems that the whole world is against us. We face hard decisions and struggle through tough days, ending up emotionally and spiritually exhausted. But listen to what David says about the Shepherd, "He restores my soul," (Psalm 23:3).

"Restore" as it appears here is translated from the original Hebrew word *shub*, and it literally means "*to turn or to bring back or to come back, the concept of turning again.*" It is the word we translate into "turn around"; also the word that we translate "repent." Jeremiah used this word over and over—he kept calling for Israel to "turn again," to come back to the Lord.

When David uses "restore" here, he is saying that when God is your shepherd, you will never reach the point of no return. Only if you die apart from Jesus Christ, never having confessed Him as Lord and Savior and repented of your sins, is it too late. But for the people of God, there is always a way back.

The Weight of Unresolved Guilt

What creates this fear of no return? The first big factor is unresolved guilt. We experience guilt over things that we've done; guilt over things that we've said; guilt over what we *haven't* done—and we don't deal with it. Instead we let it grow until it is more than we can bear and we feel like there is no hope. And that's exactly where Satan wants you.

David reveals some of his own struggle with guilt when he writes, "For my iniquities are gone over my head; as a heavy burden they weigh too much for me. My wounds grow foul and fester because of my folly. I am bent over and greatly bowed down; I go mourning all day long," (Psalm 38:4-6). David is describing the weight of sin on his life as a tremendous burden on his shoulders. He is carrying so much guilt that he is about to buckle beneath the weight of it.

There is a famous statue of the Greek god Atlas in Rockefeller Center in New York City. It weighs two tons and depicts Atlas carrying the entire heavens on his shoulders as his punishment for having defied Zeus. What I find most interesting about the statue is that while his shoulders are broad and he demonstrates tremendous strength, his knees are buckling under the immense weight of the universe. That is how guilt affects our lives—it is beyond our ability to carry.

Have you ever tried to withstand a heavy burden of guilt? There are two things about guilt you can count on: First, we all have plenty to feel guilty about. Second, we cannot get away from it. In Proverbs 20:27, Solomon said, "The spirit of man is the lamp of the Lord, searching all the innermost parts of his being." In other words, Solomon is saying that you and I have a conscience that cannot be turned on and off.

So how do we deal with it? There are six ways that we attempt to cope with guilt in our lives. The first is **denunciation**. We deny our guilt and say it does not exist. *It's not sin... it's not a big deal... I didn't do anything wrong*. When we denounce our past we essentially are trying to bury what will not stay buried. It's like something out of the horror film, *The Night of the Living Dead*. The truth is it keeps coming back to haunt us.

The second thing we often do is **minimalization**. We tell ourselves that what we did was really no big deal; there is no reason to feel bad about it. *It's so small—so trivial. I really didn't do anything that wrong. It's really no big deal... what's all the fuss about?*

Coping mechanism number three is **concession**. We concede that we are guilty and give in to the sin. If we do it again and again, after a while we get to the place where it doesn't matter anymore. There is an old Chinese proverb that says, "Commit a sin twice and it will not seem like sin anymore." We think, *Okay, I admit it's wrong, but I can't stop. So I'm just going to keep doing it and God's not going to hold me responsible because He knows I can't help it. I can't stop myself.*

Next, we **rationalize**. We point to others for validation. We tell ourselves, *Well, the law says it's fine. And everybody else is doing it. Even that church I went to says it's perfectly normal.* It might have seemed wrong before, but we rationalize that it is just an old fashioned mindset. After all, the modern world is different and we can't be expected to follow such out-of-date ideas.

The fifth thing we do is **projection**. Our culture has this one down to an art form. We project our behavior onto others and blame them for what is wrong with us. *I may be having an affair, but you know what? It's really my wife's fault because she doesn't treat me right. If she were a better wife, I wouldn't have to cheat.* Nothing is ever our fault because we project all of our guilt onto someone else.

Finally, we try to eradicate our guilt by **self-affliction**. We reach a point where we constantly beat ourselves up on the inside. We tell ourselves, *I don't deserve forgiveness. I don't deserve God's love. I don't deserve anything from God—no mercy, no grace. I'm no good—I'm just a wretch. Lower than a worm.* The truth is you can internalize guilt to the point that you make yourself sick, depressed, and angry.

Let me tell you, none of that works. Whether you do just one, or all six, it only masks the real issue. What David is saying is that if you will allow the Lord to be your shepherd, He can restore your soul. Only He can resolve your guilt.

The Power of Forgiveness

Why do we struggle so mightily with guilt in our lives? Because we don't understand forgiveness. We think, *I have prayed and prayed but nothing happens. I don't feel any different—there's no way God has forgiven me.* Fortunately, forgiveness is not based on how we feel. To truly be free from guilt, we have to know what scripture teaches about forgiveness.

It is important to understand the nature of forgiveness. Forgiveness is immediate, free, and complete. The Bible says, "When you were dead in your transgressions and the uncircumcision of your flesh, He made you alive together with Him, having forgiven us all our transgressions, having canceled out the certificate of debt consisting of decrees against us, which was hostile to us; and He has taken it out of the way, having nailed it to the cross," (Colossians 2:13-14).

Did you notice that it says, "having forgiven us *all* our transgressions..."? How did Jesus forgive us all our transgressions? He nailed them on the cross. Your sin, your guilt, your iniquity—past, present, and future—He took it and nailed it to the cross. Sounds good, right? Well how do we get there?

We have to do our part. The Bible says, "If we confess our sins, He is faithful and righteous to forgive us our sins and to cleanse us from all unrighteousness," (1 John 1:9). That's how it works: we go to Him and confess that we have sinned. And what does He do? He immediately forgives us of our sin and cleanses us from *everything*.

If you have come before the Lord and repented of your sins, but you keep stumbling over them you need to know that it is not God who is dredging them up. The Lord said, "For I will be merciful to their iniquities, and I will remember them no more," (Hebrews 8:12). He not only *forgives* our sins, He *forgets* them! God doesn't throw your past in your face. There are only two possible culprits in that situation. Number one is Satan. Scripture says he is "the accuser of the brethren." It is one of his favorite methods for keeping you paralyzed by fear.

The other one most likely to constantly remind you of your guilt is *you*. There can come a point when you are so accustomed to guilt and condemnation that you can't get past it. You mentally relive every mistake and sin over and over. But the Bible says that "Therefore there is now no condemnation for those who are in Christ Jesus," (Romans 8:1). If you find that you still struggle with something you have asked God to forgive, pull that scripture out. Read it and remind yourself and the devil that there is *no* condemnation for those who are in Christ Jesus!

The Burden of Unrelieved Grief

All of us have experienced hurt. It is a given that in this world we are going to experience hurt, loneliness, loss, sorrow, separation, and grief. Many people wonder why God created the world with so much suffering and heartache. The answer is He *didn't*. The world we have now is not the world He originally designed. Fortunately, we can thank God we have the hope of something better to come. In the meantime, the real problem comes from

unrelieved grief—when we can't move beyond our suffering—and that burden creates the fear of no return.

What causes us to grieve? There are four main ways that grief enters our lives. The first is that we grieve *because of our own actions*. We can be unkind, unfair, or mean-spirited to other people and we know it. The sad truth is that "hurting people hurt people." In our hearts, we know it's not right. And yet we can't seem to help ourselves. And so what does that do? It only creates more guilt, pain, and grief in our lives.

Secondly, we grieve *because people that we love are hurting*. We've all had someone that we love go through a difficult time. We watch them experience suffering and pain, and that causes us pain. We hurt because they are hurting; we grieve because they are grieving.

Next we grieve *because of a loss or separation*. It could be the death of a loved one or possibly a divorce. Even a less dramatic separation can be extremely difficult—the loss of a special friendship, the termination of a job, the end of a significant stage in life. And we grieve for what we had that has changed or been lost.

Finally, we grieve *because we have been hurt*. In most cases, someone has hurt us and we don't understand why. We think, *I don't understand... why did this happen to me? What did I do to deserve this pain? What did I do wrong?* And often, there is no satisfactory answer to our questions.

How do you handle the grief in your life? Where do you go when you are hurt? Many people run from one relationship to another thinking that finding another person is the answer. Others withdraw into a protective shell and lock themselves away, vowing that they will never let anyone close enough to hurt them again. But all that does is make us bitter and miserable.

Now David was a man who was well acquainted with grief. In the book of 2 Samuel, chapters 11 and 12, we read about the sad story of David and Bathsheba. David was King of Israel and had many lovely wives. But when he saw the beautiful wife of Uriah the Hittite, he coveted her for himself. He committed adultery with Bathsheba and she became pregnant. Then, when David was unable to trick Uriah into believing the child was his, David instead had him murdered on the battlefield.

After such a tangle of sin, lies, and deception, it's little wonder that David would have struggled with guilt. But because of his sin, God's judgment fell on his house and the child that Bathsheba bore him died. During this season of his life, David wrote, "Be gracious to me, O Lord, for I am in distress; My eye is wasted away from grief, my soul, and my body also," (Psalm 31:9).

David had committed adultery. He had murdered an innocent man. He had lived a lie and, as a result of his sin, his child died. In this passage of scripture he is saying, "I have cried and cried because of this. I hurt so badly that my soul and body are wasting away." Guilt will make you sick. Circumstances like these can feel overwhelming and hopeless. But it is important for us to see how David responded to his grief:

"Then it happened on the seventh day
that the child died. And the servants of

David were afraid to tell him that the
child was dead, for they said, 'Behold,
while the child was still alive, we spoke
to him and he did not listen to our voice.
How then can we tell him that the child
is dead, since he might do himself harm!'
"But when David saw that his servants
were whispering together, David per-
ceived that the child was dead; so David
said to his servants, 'Is the child dead?'
And they said, 'He is dead.'
"So David arose from the ground,
washed, anointed himself, and changed
his clothes; and he came into the house
of the Lord and worshiped. Then he
came to his own house, and when he
requested, they set food before him and
he ate.
"Then his servants said to him, 'What
is this thing that you have done? While
the child was alive, you fasted and
wept; but when the child died, you
arose and ate food.'
"He said, 'While the child was still alive,
I fasted and wept; for I said, 'Who
knows, the Lord may be gracious to me,
that the child may live.'
"But now he has died; why should I fast?

*Can I bring him back again? I will go to
him, but he will not return to me.'"*
—2 Samuel 12:18-23

First, David learned to live with what he couldn't change. He said, "I can't change what has taken place." David could not change the fact that the little baby had died. He had sinned terribly and could not undo it. All the grieving in the world will not change anything. The first step to recovery is to accept what you cannot change. I can't change my past and circumstances, and neither can you.

Next, David willed himself to worship. When word came that the child had died, David got up, cleaned himself, and went to worship before God. At that moment in his life when he hurt the most, he chose to praise God. Worship will transform your grief. He focused on what was left to him and not what was lost.

The worst thing you can do in the midst of grief is exaggerate it; allow it to become bigger than all of life. Focus on what you have and not what you have lost. God is not finished with you. That is why worship is critical in moments of despair, when you are grieving and feel that there is no return.

God has you here for a purpose, and you do not have to allow the hurt to devastate you. Instead turn your attention to what He has placed within your hands. Then you will discover, as David did, that God does restore. He is the Great Shepherd who has the ability to restore your soul.

The Cost of Unrepentant Grudges

We've talked about the impact of unresolved guilt and unrelieved grief on our lives, but there is one more thing that creates the fear of no return, and that is an unrepentant grudge. A grudge is something we feel—hatred and resentment toward another person—because of something that has been done to us. If we don't forgive that person, then we carry anger and bitterness around with us everywhere we go.

It's a fact of life—people will hurt us intentionally and unintentionally. That is not the issue; what matters is how we handle it. When we react negatively to hurt it becomes resentment and that creates bitterness. You and I cannot always choose the circumstances of life; however, we can choose how we respond to them.

The Bible says, "For anger slays the foolish man, and jealousy kills the simple," (Job 5:2). Many people *never* forgive and take deep-seated grudges to their graves. Unforgiveness will make your body sick. It will make your soul sick. It will come between you and God. And if you don't deal with it, you will be paralyzed by fear.

The ironic thing is that while resentment will paralyze you, the object of your grudge is almost always unaffected. Most likely they aren't aware of your feelings; it doesn't bother them one way or the other. You never really cross their mind. They may have moved away, or no longer come in contact with you. The offense might have occurred so long ago that they wouldn't even remember you! They have gone on with their lives—but you have not gone on with yours.

In some cases people carry a grudge against someone who has been dead for years. What is the point? Nursing that grudge every day isn't going to change their situation in eternity one bit. However, it will eat you alive.

There are three ways that we allow grudges to gain control of our lives. First, we **rehearse** them. We spend time replaying the event over and over again in our minds. After a while, we've relived it so many times that it becomes a permanent part of our thinking process.

The second thing we do is **rehash** the offense. We sit around and entertain different outcomes and scenarios. We consider the event from every angle and think, *If only I'd said this... or done that...* We mentally kick ourselves for not handling the situation differently, and determine we will never let something like that happen again.

Finally, we contemplate **revenge**. We fantasize about how we are going to pay them back, make them hurt the way they have hurt us. We want to right the wrong that was done to us. We think, *I'm going to make you pay. I'll corner you and do whatever is necessary so that you get yours. And everyone will know that you were wrong and I was right.* And really, that is the real root of a grudge—we become more concerned with being right than our relationship with God or our relationships with anyone else.

Let It Go

The Japanese surrender on September 2, 1945, aboard the U.S.S. Missouri marked the official end to World War II. But for one determined Japanese soldier, the war to end all wars did not conclude until March 5, 1974. Nearly *twenty-nine years* after V-J Day, Second Lieutenant Hiroo Onoda finally surrendered his Samurai sword and his Arisaka 99 rifle, still in operating condition.

This remarkable story began when Onoda was sent to the Philippine island of Lubang on December 26, 1944, with orders to do everything possible to hamper the enemy, including destroying the airstrip and pier at the harbor. He was also told that under no circumstances was he to surrender or take his own life.

After landing on the island, Onoda joined a Japanese unit that was already deployed there, but the other officers in the group outranked Onoda and prevented him from carrying out his assignment. As a result, U.S. and Philippine forces found it much easier to take the island on February 28, 1945. After the ensuing battle, all but Onoda and three other soldiers had either died or surrendered. Now the senior ranking officer, Onoda ordered his men to take to the hills.

For almost twenty-nine years Onoda waged a one-man war, as his three companions had either surrendered or been killed. But Onoda refused to give up. Leaflets were dropped stating that the war was over, but Onoda believed they were propaganda. Pictures and notes from family members were sent, urging him to surrender, but he ignored them. Philippine forces tried capturing him but they were unsuccessful.

Finally, a Japanese college dropout found him while hiking across Southeast Asia. Onoda told the student that he would not surrender without orders. With pictures in hand, the student returned to Japan and told the story of his encounter with Onoda. The Japanese government located Onoda's commanding officer, Major Taniguchi, and flew him to Lubang Island. The Major hiked into the jungle, met Onoda, and ordered him to surrender.

Later on, a news reporter asked Second Lieutenant Onoda what had happened to him during those twenty-nine years that he continued to fight World War II. Onoda reportedly said "Not one good thing." That is exactly what happens to us when we carry grudges and resentment, and cling to unforgiveness— not one good thing.

So, if we want to be free from fear, what do we do with unforgiveness? Job gives us the answer:

> "If you would direct your heart right and
> spread out your hand to Him, if iniquity
> is in your hand, put it far away, and do
> not let wickedness dwell in your tents;
> "Then, indeed, you could lift up your face
> without moral defect, and you would be
> steadfast and not fear.
> "For you would forget your trouble, as

*waters that have passed by, you would
remember it.*
*"Your life would be brighter than noon-
day; darkness would be like the morning.*
*"Then you would trust, because there is
hope; and you would look around and
rest securely."*

—Job 11:13-18

Job tells us to first repent and get your heart right before
God. Reach out to Him and confess the sin of unforgiveness—
that grudge you are carrying—and get rid of it. Then, forget your
trouble, "as waters that have passed by." Just pray, "Lord, it's all
water under the bridge. What that person did to me, that event
that took place in my life years ago, that hurt, whatever it was—
is over. Make me new in Jesus Christ."

David once asked the question, "Why art thou cast
down, O my soul?" (Psalm 42:5 KJV). The phrase "cast down" is
the same term that was used for a sheep that had fallen down
and was stuck on its back. Now, for a sheep, that is a life-threat-
ening situation.

When a sheep falls on its back, its legs will flail in the air
and as the blood leaves them, they quickly become numb. Then,
because of a sheep's unique physiology, gases that begin to build
up in the stomach can cause the air passage to become blocked
and the sheep will suffocate.

To save the sheep, the shepherd does not flip it over right
away, but he will lay the sheep on its side and massage its legs.

Once the blood is circulating again, he will slowly turn the sheep upright and hold it steady until its equilibrium is restored.

That is the perfect picture of what God wants to do for you. You may be living with unresolved guilt, unrelieved grief, and unrepentant grudges, but He wants to take you and hold you up until you can catch your spiritual breath. Really, that's what David is saying when he writes, "*He restores my soul...*" If you will just return to Him, God will lift you to an upright position and will restore and heal and forgive. We never need to fear to return to our Shepherd.

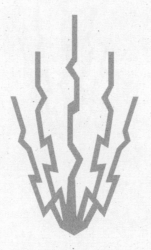

Chapter 4

AIMLESSNESS

He guides me in the paths of righteous-
ness for His name's sake.

—**Psalm 23:3b**

The spring of 2009 marked the twentieth anniversary of the Tiananmen Square protests in China, which culminated with the Tiananmen Square massacre on June 4, 1989. During that tragic event, hundreds of protestors were killed and many more severely injured as the communist Chinese government sought to crush the democratic uprising among students and other political dissidents.

Minister, writer, and former Moody Bible Institute President Joseph Stowell has told the story of meeting a Chinese man who was a young university student at the time of the massacre. As one of thousands who bought into the dream of the democracy movement, he said, "All of our hope and faith and trust was placed in the conviction that we were going to take over the nation and make it a democratic society." But when Chinese troops killed the protesters and put down the rebellion, it destroyed their dream. For countless Chinese people their one hope for a better life was shattered.

As a result, thousands of distraught Chinese students committed suicide. Their despair was so overwhelming that they believed they had nothing left to live for. They no longer had a purpose; they had no direction in life.

The young Chinese man was no different. Looking for answers, he remembered an English teacher back at the university who was a Christian. He and the other students had often mocked the man because he believed in God. But in his despair, he sought out that English professor and asked about the God he believed in. As a result, the young student accepted Jesus Christ as Lord and Savior. He went on to graduate and was assigned to teach at one of the universities in China.

Like his English professor before him, as he taught he found ways to share his faith, and soon others came to know Jesus. He would throw parties in a nearby hotel and the Christian students would invite their unsaved friends. During these parties, different people would stand up and share their testimony of how Jesus had changed their lives, and inevitably someone would make the decision to trust Christ. Then they would lock the door, go into the bathroom, and baptize them in the bathtub.

That young professor revealed that right now, on every single university campus in China, there is an active and thriving group of believers. Despite the oppression of communism, they are sold out to Jesus Christ and are actively sharing their faith as best they can. More than twenty years later, there continues to be a great harvest from the ashes of Tiananmen Square.

What is the lesson of this story? First, it is the perfect illustration of how God often moves behind the scenes, accomplishing His will even in the most difficult circumstances. When situations or events occur that we think are devastating to the advancement of the Kingdom, it is important that we not give in to despair. God is always at work in ways we do not see.

Secondly, God will guide you even if you are completely lost, just like He did this young Chinese student. Even when we suffer from complete hopelessness, if our hearts are open to the leading of the Holy Spirit, He will direct us to the answer to all of life's disappointments, which is Jesus Christ.

A Guide for the Journey

Many believers are going through life without any understanding of their purpose. At one time they had dreams and goals for the future. But when things don't work out exactly as planned, and when dreams go unfulfilled, they can leave a lingering sense of aimlessness behind.

Aimlessness—the lack of direction, purpose, and hope— is a paralyzing condition in the church today. It is a sad truth that so many Christians are living as though they have no direction in their lives whatsoever. But those who know Jesus have no reason to ever feel aimless, because the Bible says that the Shepherd guides us.

David writes, "*He guides me* in the paths of righteousness for His name's sake," (Psalm 23:3b). Now we've already talked about how the Shepherd "leads us beside quiet waters." In the English language, we often use "lead" and "guide" interchangeably. But here "guides" comes from a different Hebrew word with a separate meaning.

The word "lead" involves the concept of a destination. A leader has a specific goal. *The Shepherd leads* me beside still waters. He leads me to a place; he has a destination in mind. "Guide," on the other hand, is about the process. It's about the journey. *He guides me* in the paths of righteousness. He is walking beside me; guiding me all along the way.

Now we see this repeated throughout the Old Testament. Moses said that God not only leads, He also guides, "In Your loving-kindness You have led the people whom You have redeemed; In Your strength You have guided them to Your holy habitation," (Exodus 15:13). Isaiah 58:11 says, "the Lord will continually guide you." Do you see that? He is *always* guiding you. He is always there.

Roadblocks to Receiving

You see the issue is not whether God *can* guide us, or *will* guide us, He can and He will. The question is will we *allow* Him to guide us? How many times have we thought, "*I don't know what to do... if only God would just give me some guidance. If only the Lord would lead me I would follow.*" Then why don't we seemingly receive the guidance that we need?

There are six significant roadblocks to receiving God's guidance in our lives. First, we **question God's intentions** toward us. In truth, we really doubt God's motives. We get into a fearful situation, or we lose a job, or perhaps our health starts to suffer, and we wonder "*God, what are You doing to me? Why are You allowing this to happen*?" We automatically blame Him for our problems, and we become suspicious of God instead of putting our full and complete trust in Him.

Did you know Job did just the opposite? Job arguably suffered more than any other man in the Bible next to Jesus, but the worse things got, the more trust he seemed to have in the Lord. He said, "Though He slay me, I will hope in Him," (Job 13:15). Even death by God's hand wasn't enough to make Job question His goodness. How many of us could say the same?

Secondly, we don't experience God's guidance because **we believe we need more** than what God can provide for us. Now most of us would admit that God has met our basic needs, and He has. But what we really want is for God to also meet our **desires**. I experienced this as a father, particularly when my children were teenagers. They would say, "Dad ...listen, I've just got to have more than what you are giving me."

We say essentially the same thing to God. "Well, God you know, I'm not satisfied with you just meeting my needs—there are so many things out there I want." And we start to question whether we are ever going to experience richness or fullness in this life; or find completeness or satisfaction. We begin to view Him as a miserly benefactor, dispensing stale crumbs when we really want meat.

What a distorted view of a heavenly Father who gave everything that He had on a cross at Calvary to save us! The apostle Paul wrote:

> *"But God, being rich in mercy, because of His great love with which He loved us, even when we were dead in our transgressions, made us alive together with Christ (by grace you have been saved), and raised us up with Him, and seated us with Him in the heavenly places in Christ Jesus, so that in the ages to come He might show the surpassing riches of His grace in kindness toward us in Christ Jesus."*
>
> —Ephesians 2:4-7

What Paul is saying is that for all of eternity, Jesus is going to hold you up as an example of His goodness and kindness. He's going to pour out His riches upon us—and not just a little! "Now to Him who is able to do far more abundantly beyond all that we ask or think, according to the power that works within us," (Ephesians 3:20). Paul is saying, "Do you think God is a miser? God wants to heap all the riches of heaven on your life. And He will do it beyond your ability to ask or think." But God can't guide you if you think that He won't give you what you need.

The next hindrance to receiving God's guidance is that *we place other priorities above our loyalty to the Lord*. We'll say, "Now God, listen, I'll take care of this area. My work is going so well... my business is growing... and things are going great with this relationship... I've got to handle all this stuff, I've got it under control. But, now the other 90 percent of my life, God you can guide me there." But God will not be satisfied with 90 percent of your life. Billy Graham says, "If He's not Lord of *all*, He's not Lord *at all*." And he's exactly right—if you aren't going to give Him 100 percent of yourself, then you can't expect His guidance in any area of your life.

Number four, *we try and conform God to our image*. We are particularly guilty of doing this in the church. Have you ever stopped to think about how much we get wrapped up in the traditions we have created? We get to the point where we begin to associate the tradition with God Himself. We think that's the only way God can work.

The Pharisees did the very same thing. When Jesus came, the first century Jew knew exactly who Jesus was. The Old

Testament was so full of Jesus—who and what He would be—that the educated Pharisees recognized him. One Pharisee named Nicodemus said, "Rabbi, we know that You have come from God as a teacher; for no one can do these signs that You do unless God is with him," (John 3:2). And yet the Jews rejected Jesus and said, "you don't fit into our box of tradition, and if you won't become conformed to *our* image, then we would rather kill you than change how we do things." Let me tell you something—if you try to conform God to your image, He will not be able to guide you.

Next, ***we resist His correction***. When there is sin in a believer's life, God works every angle to make us aware of our sin and bring sufficient pressure on us to repent of it. "For whom the Lord loves He reproves, even as a father corrects the son in whom He delights," (Proverbs 3:12). It is important that we understand that the reproof of God, the chastening of God, the discipline of God—is God's love toward us. And yet so often we resist and push away the loving, disciplining hand of God. "*I don't want that in my life. I don't want to be corrected. I don't want to change. Just leave me alone.*"

I remember clearly the last time my mother gave me a spanking. Now my mama is a tiny woman, only about 89 pounds, but she had a belt in her right hand and spanked me. And I just stood there and stared at her. In fact, I said something like, "Well, go ahead, hit me." Do you know what I was doing? I was resisting her discipline. I would not submit to her correction in my life.

My mother's next words were, "Your dad is coming home soon." All 235 pounds, 52-inch chest, of a former Golden Gloves boxer—judgment was on the way. The chastening hand of God is

His love in operation in our lives, and when we resist His correction, God cannot guide us. But He will eventually send judgment. Daddy's coming home.

Lastly, the final roadblock to receiving God's guidance in our lives is that *we eliminate righteous reminders* in our lives. So often when we allow sin in our lives, we discover that being in church, listening to the teaching and preaching of God's word, or being around other Christians is awkward and irritating. When we have unconfessed and hidden sin in our lives, our first instinct is usually to put as much distance as possible between ourselves and the things of God.

The question we have to ask ourselves is do we *really* want God's guidance? We can come to the place where we rely completely on self-direction rather than the loving, guiding hand of God. But self-direction always results in aimlessness. We can't have it both ways—we have to make a choice between God's way or our own.

Choosing Divine Direction

Now, David says, "He guides me in the paths of righteousness for His name's sake." At first glance it seems obvious that He would guide us in "paths of righteousness." Does that mean paths that are pure? Yes, God is not going to lead us into impurity. Paths that are moral? Yes, God does not lead us into immorality. Paths that are holy? Of course, He is a holy God, where else would He guide us? But it also means something much more.

The Hebrew word used here for "path" is the same as the English word "track." When someone goes hunting, they look for animal tracks—deer, turkey, whatever they are pursuing—in order to locate their prey. So this scripture could also be read to say, "He guides me in the *tracks* of righteousness."

A native shepherd in the land of Palestine is an expert at reading tracks. If you were to travel to Israel, you would notice that the land is engraved with countless paths and trails leading in all directions. Now, some are made by sheep, others by predatory animals, and still others by humans. But as we've mentioned before, sheep have no sense of direction and they have absolutely no idea which path to follow. The sheep need the guidance of their shepherd.

In the book of Psalms we read, "*Your way was in the sea and Your paths in the mighty waters, and Your footprints may not be known. You led Your people like a flock by the hand of Moses and Aaron,*" (Psalm 77:19-20). What the Psalmist is saying is that God can see roadways in the ocean. Do you realize that this was written almost 1,500 years before anyone understood what currents were? Long before any scientists knew about the gulf stream or other similar geological patterns, the Word of God talks about it. Isn't that amazing?

Like a shepherd with his sheep, the Lord could see a clear path through the ocean and He chose the right one because He knew it was best for the children of Israel. Can you imagine being able to see a clear path in the ocean? Only God is capable of that. He sees what no one else is able to see. In the same way that the shepherd is able to decipher which path in the maze of a hundred is the right one to take, God knows exactly which path you should take.

More than anything else, God wants to be your guide in life. He created you; He knows you better than anyone else—even better than you know yourself. We spend so much of life trying to be something we are not, trying to go the way that seems best to us. That is why we struggle with aimlessness. God is the one who has already seen the path of your life and knows where to guide you. He sees what you cannot see.

The Guidance of God

So if we want God to guide us, how do we receive His direction? There are four simple ways that God will guide us. First is through the *Word of God*. This is the single, most important tool that God uses to guide our lives. You don't have to wonder, *How am I supposed to live?* God has given us instructions on exactly how He wants us to live in His Word. He tells us how we are to talk, love, and take care of ourselves. How to handle our money, function as a family, serve as an employee, and take care of our neighbors. He tells us what we're supposed to do and what we're not supposed to do. Most of what we struggle with is pointless struggle because God has already addressed those issues in His Word.

The second way God guides us is through the *Holy Spirit*. Now in my experience, I have found that most people fit into one of two extremes when it comes to the Holy Spirit. They are either overboard emotionally or they are scared to death of the Holy Spirit. In John 15:26 we read, "When the Helper comes, whom I will send to you from the Father, that is the Spirit of truth who proceeds from the Father, He will testify about me."

Do you see that? He is the Helper, the Spirit of truth, sent from God the Father. He gives us guidance. Every believer knows what it is like to be nudged by the Holy Spirit as He moves us in one direction or the other. He does it through gentle prompting, and what He prompts us to do is never contrary to the Word of God.

Next, God uses **Godly counsel** to guide our lives. The Bible says, "For by wise guidance you will wage war, and in abundance of counselors there is victory," (Proverbs 24:6). Now every church has its share of self-proclaimed "counselors," but I've discovered in my life that true godly counsel usually comes from people who don't publicize it. They are believers living quietly under the radar who give evidence of godliness in their lives. Let me tell you something, there is a great deal of difference between those who inflict their opinion upon others and those who are wise, Godly counselors. We need to heed **wise** Godly counsel, and God will use that to guide us along the right path.

Finally, God also uses **our own personalities**. All of us are unique creations of God—some a little more unique than others! Now, the problem for most of us is that we spend our lives trying to be somebody else. We worry about what other people will think of us, when we would be so much better off just being ourselves.

I remember one day early in my ministry a dear friend gave me a great piece of advice. He looked at me and said, "You just be wonderful you." That has stuck with me throughout the years. It's practical too—if you will be who God created you to be, instead of someone else, then you are much less likely to take detours off the path that God has chosen for you.

Practical Principles

Sometimes things are not always cut and dried. Even when we desperately want to follow God's will, sometimes we just aren't sure what He wants us to do. It can be hard to see things clearly. Paul writes to the church in Corinth, "For now we see in a mirror dimly, but then face to face; now I know in part, but then I will know fully just as I also have been fully known," (1 Corinthians 13:12). If you are struggling with a decision or aren't sure what you are supposed to do next, don't allow fear to paralyze you. Instead, follow these four practical principles:

First, when a decision has to be made and you cannot find a clear scriptural directive, *lean on the Holy Spirit* to guide you as you proceed. Sometimes we have to take a step of faith and say, "Holy Spirit, I yield to your Lordship and I'll let you work it out."

Secondly, feelings of euphoria do not necessarily confirm God's leading. Too often we *mistake an emotional response* as evidence of God's will. In fact, being obedient to God more often brings difficulty than bliss.

Next is perhaps the hardest—**wait on God**. So many people get stressed out about God's will and God's timing. We have the mindset that everything has to be done *right now*. But God's timetable usually is very different from our own. Instead of rushing headlong into something because we are anxious, we need to learn to wait on God.

Finally, **take comfort in God's sovereignty**. Many times we become distraught when we make a wrong decision. But we need to understand that it isn't the end of the world. In fact, God even manages to turn our mistakes into blessings. Paul writes to the Romans, "And we know that God causes all things to work together for good to those who love God, to those who are called according to His purpose," (Romans 8:28). God is not out to *get* you—He is here *for* you. God knows you are searching for His will, and He will work everything out for your good.

There is no greater tragedy than to finish this life without having known or fulfilled the plan that God created us for. Too often, we choose to go our own way, and the result is always aimlessness and despair.

But if you will allow Him, God will guide you in the path that is right for your life. David explains God's guidance in Psalm 37, "The steps of a man are ordered by the Lord, and He delights in his way. When he falls, he will not be hurled headlong, because the Lord is the One who holds his hand," (Psalm 37:23-24).

The Lord is my shepherd… He guides me in the paths that are right for me.

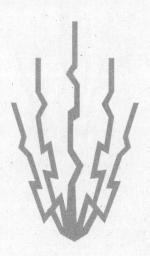

Chapter 5

THROUGH
THE VALLEYS

Even though I walk through the valley of the shadow of death, I fear no evil, for You are with me; Your rod and Your staff, they comfort me.

—Psalm 23:4

The land of Israel has a unique and distinctive topography that is into four main geographic regions: the Coastal Plain, the Central Highlands, the Jordan Rift Valley, and the Negev Desert. The Mediterranean Coastal Plain is fertile and humid, known for its citrus and viniculture. East of the coastal plain lies the Central Highland Region—featuring the mountains and hills of Upper Galilee and Lower Galilee in the north, and the Samarian Hills to the south, which are dotted with numerous small, fertile valleys. South of Jerusalem are the mainly barren hills of Judea.

The Jordan Rift Valley is an elongated depression that includes the Jordan River, Jordan Valley, the Sea of Galilee, and the Dead Sea—the lowest land elevation on Earth. Rising sharply to more than a half a mile both to the east and to the west, the rift is a rugged land feature that accommodates only a few narrow paved roads and difficult mountain tracks. Finally, the Negev Desert covers nearly 7,500 square miles—more than half of Israel's total land area.

The geographical features and characteristics of the land have always played an important role in the Bible, ever since God spoke to Abraham and said,

> "Go forth from your country, and from your relatives and from your father's house, to the land which I will show you; and I will make you a great nation, and I will bless you, and make your name great; and so you shall be a blessing; and I will bless those who bless you, and the one who curses you I will curse. And in you all the families of the earth will be blessed."
>
> So Abram went forth as the Lord had spoken to him; and Lot went with him. Now Abram was seventy-five years old when he departed from Haran.
>
> Abram took Sarai his wife and Lot his nephew, and all their possessions which

*they had accumulated, and the persons
which they had acquired in Haran, and
they set out for the land of Canaan; thus
they came to the land of Canaan.
Abram passed through the land as far as
the site of Shechem, to the oak of
Moreh. Now the Canaanite was then in
the land.
The Lord appeared to Abram and said,
"To your descendants I will give this
land." So he built an altar there to the
Lord who had appeared to him.
Then he proceeded from there to the
mountain on the east of Bethel, and
pitched his tent, with Bethel on the west
and Ai on the east; and there he built an
altar to the Lord and called upon the
name of the Lord.*

—Genesis 12:1-8

Abraham and his descendants had a long and difficult
struggle to take possession of the land God had promised
them—a struggle that still continues to this day. But the
significance of these places is more than just a historical
travelogue—they also illustrate spiritual lessons that apply to
our own lives.

You see, Israel is filled with mountains and valleys, and
the interesting thing is that these landmarks are named for

important events that occurred there. As we read the Old Testament, we find that there are a multitude of valleys whose names aptly describe the long-suffering history of the Jewish people:

- **Valley of Achor** – *trouble, calamity* – Joshua 7:24
- **Valley of Hinnom** – *lamentation* – Joshua 15:8
- **Valley of the Rephaim** – *giants* – Joshua 15:8
- **Valley of Baca** – *weeping* – Psalm 84:6
- **Valley of the Slaughter** – Jeremiah 7:32
- **Valley of the Dead Bodies** – Jeremiah 31:40
- **Valley of Jehoshaphat** – *judgment* – Joel 3:2
- **Valley of Decision** – Joel 3:14

No matter where the inhabitants of Israel traveled, they encountered mountains, hills, and dangerous valleys. And just like the children of Abraham, we experience valleys in life. We have all been in the valley of decision; the valley of weeping; the valley of calamity and trouble. But no valley in scripture is as familiar as the valley David writes about: "*Even though I walk through the valley of the shadow of death...*" (Psalm 23:4).

We've talked about how the Lord is our Shepherd. He leads us to green pastures and quiet waters. He guides us in the paths of righteousness. But here David is saying that there will be situations in life that are so treacherous and dark that they can only be described as the valleys of the shadow of death.

Now, let's be honest—we don't like the sound of that. In the Word of God, valleys symbolize darkness and difficulty. They are times of trouble and struggle. And when we find ourselves in those places, we cry out to God, pleading *"God, why are You doing this? Why is this happening? Why did You lead me here? I don't like this. This is too hard."*

Unfortunately, the valleys of life are unavoidable. But even though we all must pass through them, they don't have to be valleys of fear. They don't have to destroy us. There can be encouragement and peace in the valleys of life. The truth is we encounter God in those places in a way that is closer and clearer than at any other time in our lives.

The Characteristics of the Valley

The Shepherd will guide us in paths of righteousness, but those paths are not always easy. Jesus said, "In the world you have tribulation, but take courage; I have overcome the world," (John 16:33). It is important that we not equate righteousness with ease. To stand for what is right will cost you. The path to the peace of God, the righteousness of God, and the holiness of God will always lead through valleys of tribulation. It's through these valleys—hard times of struggle and difficulty—that God moves us to where He wants us to be.

Notice that David said, "Even though I walk...." He does not say *if* I walk, but rather he writes as though it is a foregone conclusion that there would be times when he would pass through this valley. In fact, in a literal sense, he probably already had.

Remember, as a boy David was the shepherd of his father's flock. Depending on the time of year, a shepherd would have to move his sheep from one geographical area to another. In the springtime, the sheep would graze down near the Jordan River, but when summer came the shepherds would turn their flocks to the highlands, toward the hills where the temperatures were cooler and where the grass was more plentiful.

It is quite likely that David himself had moved his father's sheep from those lowlands up into the highlands. And not far from Jericho there is a deep valley that runs up toward Jerusalem, known as the Valley of the Shadow of Death. About four-and-a-half miles long and as deep as 1,500 feet, there are some places in that valley that are only twelve to fourteen feet wide. The passageway is so narrow, two flocks could not possibly pass each other going different directions, so the shepherds know that they must travel one direction in the morning, and the opposite way in the evening.

There are three important characteristics that are helpful to understand about this valley. First, it is **difficult**. This is not a wide, gently rolling meadow that we might see nestled in one of America's mountain ranges. Instead, the valley is more like a deep and narrow canyon with some of the harshest terrain imaginable. The valley floor is rough and uneven, littered with potholes and marred by deep trenches—seven or eight feet deep—that have been carved out over time by the regular sudden, torrential bursts of rain. It is not smooth, it is not level, and the way is difficult. So often life is just like that. We have to go through a narrow, confining place where the ground is dangerous and unpredictable and we must watch every step we take.

Second, the valley is **depressing**. Why did the Hebrew people name this the Valley of the Shadow of Death? There is probably nothing quite as ominous as what "death" implies. But in the original Hebrew, this word "death" means a darkness or gloom. In fact, the valley itself is so narrow and deep that it is constantly shrouded in darkness—the sun's rays cannot penetrate the mountain walls to reach the valley floor.

Catherine Booth, the wife of the founder of the Salvation Army, struggled for years with depression and when describing it said, "Darkness gathers thicker than ever around the path I tread, and doubt, gloom, melancholy, and despair." We will walk through valleys in life where it will seem like the darkness is almost tangible. It will seem as if the shadows of defeat and failure hang over you; as though the very shadow of death itself is closing in around you.

But, the good news is the valley is also **passable**. Listen to what David said, "Even though I walk *through* the valley of the shadow of death, I fear no evil, for You are with me." Do you see that? He said that he would walk *through* it—not succumb to it. The valley is not certain doom and destruction; it is not a death sentence. He was not going to sit down and give up. He was not going to die there. He was confident that God would take him through.

Do you know what God is doing when He guides us through the valley? He is eliminating our fear. Look again at what David wrote, "*I fear no evil*, for You are with me." It is in the valley that our faith is built and proved. It is in the valley that God teaches us and builds our character. We are usually most concerned with our comfort. But God is really not interested in our comfort—He is interested in our character. If we are going to be more like Christ, then we are going to have to go through more of what Christ experienced and encountered.

Did Christ avoid suffering? No. Then why do you think it is strange when you suffer? Was Christ exempted from loneliness? No. Then why do you think you won't feel lonely? Was Christ free from trials and tribulations? No. Then you will not be free from them either. Was Jesus ever prejudged, mistreated, and rejected? Yes. Then you can expect it as well.

One of God's purposes in leading us through the valley is to teach us to trust Him, to eliminate the stronghold of fear in our life, "So that the proof of your faith, being more precious than gold which is perishable, even though tested by fire, may be found to result in praise and glory and honor at the revelation of Jesus Christ," (1 Peter 1:7).

Preparation for the Valley

The good news is that since we know valleys are coming, we are able to prepare ourselves now for what lies ahead. I'm certain David was accustomed to thinking about taking his flock of sheep through the valleys and what was necessary for them to make it safely through. Let's look at this scripture again, *"Even though I walk through the valley of the shadow of death, I fear no evil, for You are with me; Your rod and Your staff, they comfort me,"* (Psalm 23:4). In this one sentence, he gives us three critical steps for personal preparation.

First, we must ***refuse to become discouraged***. David says, "I fear no evil." Listen, God never intended for the believer to be ruled and troubled by fear. David doesn't deny that evil exists—he simply refuses to fear it. Why? Because he knows that God is more powerful than anything that could ever come against him. The apostle Paul wrote, "For God has not given us a spirit of timidity, but of power and love and discipline," (2 Timothy 1:7). When we place our confidence in the Shepherd there is no room for fear.

What happens when we have confidence in the Shepherd? We *walk* through the valley. We do not run in a panic, or stumble through in confusion. We do not work ourselves into an emotional frenzy. David says he will "walk through it." That implies that there is a choice in how we respond.

Secondly, we must ***recognize God's presence***. One of my favorite passages of scripture is found in Isaiah 43:2, "When you pass through the waters, I will be with you; and through the rivers, they will not overflow you. When you walk through the fire, you will not be scorched, nor will the flame burn you." No matter what we face, God is with us. That is the same promise that David is speaking of here when he says, "I fear no evil, *for You are with me*."

Now, let's look at something interesting about the grammar that David uses. For the first three verses of this Psalm, David writes, "*He* makes me... *He* leads me... *He* restores my soul." Then, in verse four, David stops talking *about* God and starts talking *to* Him: "*You* are with me; *Your* rod and *Your* staff, they comfort me."

It is in the valleys of life where we come face to face with God. It is in the valleys where the ultimate becomes the intimate; where theory becomes truth. You no longer want to just talk *about* God—you want to talk *with* God. It is in the valley that God reveals His presence and you realize you are not alone.

Finally, David tells us that we must **rely on God's protection**. He says, "*Your rod and Your staff, they comfort me.*" Now, we don't see rods and staffs very much these days, but they were critical tools for shepherding. The rod was a heavy stick with a knot or a root on the end of it. The shepherd could throw that thing in much the same way as an American Indian would throw a tomahawk. They were very accurate and effective for protecting the sheep from predators.

We are more familiar with the staff, since it often appears in Christmas pageants, which is essentially a tall stick with a hook on the end. Shepherds use the staff to help them navigate difficult or uneven terrain, and to guide the sheep. The shepherd can reach out with the crook to move the sheep away from a dangerous situation, pull a sheep closer, or lift a sheep up—rescuing the animal by drawing it to himself.

David writes that he is comforted by the Shepherd's rod and staff. Why? Because he knows the lengths that a shepherd will go to in order to protect the sheep. He knows how those tools are used and understands the significance of the Shepherd carrying them. As His sheep, we need to walk through the valley in complete confidence and trust that God is with us and He will protect us.

Don't Be Afraid of the Dark

Regardless of the weather conditions, the Valley of the Shadow of Death is awash in shadows. The sun may be shining brightly in a clear sky overhead, but on the floor of the valley, it is always gloomy and dark. It would be easy to become overwhelmed, to begin to believe that the whole world is full of darkness and light will never return again. But those shadows are deceiving.

Shadows always appear larger than life. Think about it ... when you see your shadow in front of you on the street, doesn't it reach far beyond your actual size? Those things in life that can seem so threatening and ominous always appear bigger than they are in reality.

Honestly, it isn't very rational that we are afraid of the dark. After all, shadows cannot hurt you. They may be large and the darkness may be unsettling, but they are not tangible. When was the last time someone was hurt by a shadow? In fact, when we walk along the street and the shadow of a big truck passes over us we pay it no attention. Why? Because shadows have no substance.

Remember, wherever there are shadows, there is also light. In fact, without light, shadows would not exist. Light must encounter the darkness for a shadow to be created. Jesus said, "I am the light of the world." Whenever we find ourselves in the valley and fearful of the shadows that stretch out before us, the best thing we can do is turn our back on the shadows and face the Light. All fear and anxiety will fade away if we follow the advice of the hymnist:

Turn your eyes upon Jesus,
Look full in His wonderful face;
And the things of earth will grow
strangely dim,
In the light of His glory and grace.

Chapter 6

GOD'S RESPONSE
TO OUR HURT

You prepare a table before me in the presence of my enemies; You have anointed my head with oil; my cup overflows.

—Psalm 23:5

I'll never forget the day I got married. Surrounded by family and friends, my wife, Debbie, and I committed our lives to one another before God at four o'clock on a Sunday afternoon. When a young couple marries, it isn't unusual for people to offer lots of well-meaning advice and guidance, and we certainly received our share. But my father said something to me that I have never forgotten after all these years. He said, "Son, let me tell you something. Marriage can be more like heaven on earth than anything else. Or, marriage can be more like hell on earth than anything else. You will determine which you have."

My dad was on to something, and in a general sense, his advice applies to all of our relationships. For the source of the greatest joy in our lives is also the source of the deepest hurt and pain—*people*. God created us with a need to interact with and rely on others. He ordered the world so that we would be born into a family, contribute to our community, and be connected with other believers. There is simply no avoiding it. We are connected to mothers, fathers, siblings, children, best friends, husbands, wives, co-workers, pastors—and all of these relationships have the potential to strengthen and bless us. But they also can cause us pain—whether intentionally inflicted or not.

We all struggle with this part of life. We get hurt and we hurt other people. It is inevitable. Unfortunately, it isn't the hurt itself that does the greatest damage, but rather how we respond to it. So what should we do when someone hurts us? There are many appropriate ways to react—first among them being to forgive. But more often than not, we respond in the wrong way that only creates more pain and fear in our lives.

There are five things you should never do when you are hurt. First, *do not ignore it*. I like to call this the "John Wayne approach." Now I love John Wayne. He was the ultimate man's man. Bite the bullet; suffer in silence, and all that. How many times did he get shot, but he would get right back up and go after it again? A normal person would cower behind a tree. Get behind a rock and stay down. But he would just keep walking into the firestorm. Why? Because he was John Wayne.

So many times we suffer needlessly because we choose to ignore what has happened to us. *If I don't think about it, it will go away.* Or we try to deny it, *What hurt? Nobody hurt me.* Or we minimize it, *Oh, it really isn't any big deal.* But let me tell you something. An ignored hurt never heals. It just keeps aching and festering under the surface.

Secondly, **do not run from it**. If the first example was John Wayne, this response is Don Knotts—otherwise known as Barney Fife from *The Andy Griffith Show*. His claim to fame was his tremendous gift for physical comedy, particularly the amazing range of his facial expressions. He could convey comical fear and insecurity like no one else. His response in stressful situations was often, "Run! Retreat!" The perfect Mr. Chicken.

Now, to want to run away from conflict is just human nature. We think, *If I just get away from it, I'll be okay. I'll just run away from my problems and from the people who have hurt me.* The problem is that running away never solves anything. It only leads to deeper issues.

Third, **do not try to hide it**. So many of us wear a mask that we hide behind whenever we go to work or to church, or spend time with family and friends. Only when we are alone do we dare to remove the facade. We don't want anyone to see that we've been hurt. We don't want to admit that we have struggles and pain. This is especially true within the church.

How many times have our friends or family members sensed something was wrong and tried to reach out? They'll ask, "How are you doing?" And we give the standard response, "Oh, just fine thanks!" We downplay the situation and act like everything is wonderful, when we know it's not. But the Bible says, "Therefore, confess your sins one to another, and pray for one another, so that you may be healed ..." (James 5:16). Now some-times, our problems are the result of our own sin, but other times we have been hurt through no fault of our own. Yet we still resist being open and honest—we don't want to be judged.

The best thing to do is confess our hurt and pain, as well as our sin. But who should we confess to? James goes on to answer that question, "Therefore, confess your sins to one another, and pray for one another so that you may be healed. *The effective prayer of a righteous man can accomplish much.*" This is so important—don't confess to just anyone. Find a "right-eous man," a mature, strong believer you can trust. Revealing what you are really going through is the beginning step toward healing. If you'll just lower the mask and be real, then God can deal with the hurt.

Next, ***do not worry about it***. We do so love to fret and stew and worry, don't we? We've already learned about the ef-fect worry can have on our lives. But when we add worry to the mixture of hurt and pain, it only complicates the problem. Re-member—the hurt itself is not the biggest issue. How we deal with hurt in our lives is what makes things better or worse. And worrying about what has been done to us accomplishes two things. First, it increases our misery exponentially. Second, it al-ways magnifies the problem, the hurt, or the injury. It always makes things worse.

Finally, ***do not resent it***. Now, this is a big one. So often hurt leads to anger, bitterness, self-pity, and deep-seated resent-ment. What happens when we allow resentment to take over? It turns one negative event into a lifetime of drama and suffering.

Bitterness begins to take root in our hearts, and causes far more damage than the original offense ever did.

We can't afford to give bitterness a place to grow. Hebrews tells us, "See to it that no one comes short of the grace of God; that no root of bitterness springing up causes trouble, and by it many be defiled," (Hebrews 12:15). Do you know what the word "defiled" means? It means *to be stained.*

Are you familiar with the dye packs that banks often put in their money in case of a robbery? At some point after the money is taken, the dye pack explodes. And everything that is nearby will get covered with permanent ink—including the money. It won't wash off. No amount of scrubbing can remove it.

That is exactly what the writer of Hebrews is telling us. He's saying, "At some point when you allow bitterness into your life and it takes root, it is going to explode and color everything." It will color how you see your wife, your children, your church, your job, even how you see God. People who are full of bitterness eventually begin to believe that God is bitter and judgmental and angry—just like them.

None of these responses will ever deal with the pain in our hearts—they simply keep the wounds open and fresh. Rather than receiving God's healing, so many of us choose to allow something that has happened in our past to control our present and determine our future.

Let God Defend You

We have talked about what *not* to do when we are hurt … but what is the *right* response? In Psalm 23, David shares with us the three steps God takes when our spirits have been crushed and our hearts have been wounded.

First, he says, "You prepare a table before me in the presence of my enemies." When a shepherd would move a flock into a new pasture, the first thing he would do is prepare the land for the sheep. He would walk over every square inch of land in order to eliminate any threat to the sheep's well being. This would include finding any poisonous plants and predatory animals—including snakes. There is a brown adder that is native to the Middle East that is notorious for coming up out of its hole and biting sheep on their noses. So the shepherd would find the snake holes and pour oil around the openings and a little down into the holes to prevent the snakes from attacking the sheep.

What is interesting here is that David has changed the metaphor he uses from sheep being cared for by their shepherd, to that of a guest at a banquet where God is the host. The imagery is certainly fitting when you consider the events of David's life. There were many times that he sat at the king's table and feasted in the presence of his enemy—Saul, the king himself. David was beloved by everyone except the king he served. In fact, Saul wanted to kill him. Yet despite Saul's animosity and murderous intentions, David experienced the protection of God.

The best position that you can take when you are hurt is the one of patience and trust. Allow the Lord time and opportunity to protect, heal, and defend you. In his letter to the Romans, Paul said, "Never take your own revenge, beloved, but leave room for the wrath of God, for it is written, 'Vengeance is mine, I will repay,' says the Lord," (Romans 12:19).

That goes against every natural instinct we have. We want to fight back, to stand up and defend ourselves. But Jesus said essentially the same thing, "But I say to you who hear, love your enemies, do good to those who hate you, bless those who curse you, pray for those who mistreat you," (Luke 6:27-28). Why? If we will just obey God and wait on His timing, He will prepare a feast of honor for us in the presence of our enemies. If we will let Him work on our behalf, He will fight our battles for us.

Let God Minister To You

The next step David shares is, "*You have anointed my head with oil...*" This also speaks to the work of the shepherd, for oil was a very important tool that served many uses in the field.

The shepherd would mix olive oil with sulfur and different spices and rub it all over the animals' heads. The first purpose was to protect the sheep. This is not a very pleasant picture to think about, but a sheep does not have a tail like a horse or a cow does to swat pests away. So flies are able to land on a sheep's nose or ears and lay their eggs. Then, when the eggs hatch it drives an animal crazy. An attentive shepherd would use the oil to prevent an infestation of parasites and insects. Secondly, the shepherd used the oil to soothe and heal any existing wounds. That is what God does for us. "He heals the brokenhearted and binds up their wounds," (Psalm 147:3).

Once you have forgiven someone who has hurt you, it does not mean that all of the hurt disappears. Healing takes time. That is something that most of us don't understand. Forgiveness is instant, but restoration takes time. It may take weeks, or months, or longer. Perhaps you have been hurt because of infidelity by your mate, or by the pain of a divorce. Perhaps you were molested as a child, or have gone through the awful trauma of an abortion, and you have never been able to get past the pain of those experiences. It takes time to be healed of those hurts. Forgiveness is a critical first step, but all of the pain does not go away immediately.

Instead, God faithfully ministers to our needs and binds our wounds. But too often we are like little children with a band-aid—we keep ripping the band-aid off too soon to take a look at what's underneath, and when we do that we open the wound all over again. We have to allow God the opportunity and time to soothe the deep wounds of life.

There are several ways that God brings us healing. The first is *fellowship*. Whether you attend a small fellowship group or Bible study, or simply gather informally with other believers, you need to have regular personal contact and support from others who know the Lord.

Prayer is equally important. When you are hurt, either you talk it out with God or you will take it out on yourself and those closest to you. It's no accident that the Psalms are so full of heartfelt emotion. They are the expression of David's heart—all of his joys and sorrows, victories and defeats—that he shares with his God.

There is nothing quite like **worship** to bring healing for our pain. Church is not about any one person or minister. It's not about being entertained. Instead, when you engage the Lord through music, praise, and hearing the Word of God presented, God begins to speak to your heart and heals the wounds.

And finally, the fourth thing God uses is **ministry**. Nothing brings healing quite like doing something for others. No matter what you have been through, there is someone else that is suffering from the same pain—or worse. And no one is better qualified to understand those problems than *you*. If we allow God to use us to show His compassion and love, then He will bring healing in our own lives.

We've talked about the fact that healing takes time. Just like when we recover from a serious physical injury or surgery, there are specific stages in the healing process. The first stage is sedation, when the medical staff is trying to keep you still and quiet after a medical procedure. This does not usually last very long. In fact, the second stage begins almost immediately when the nurse comes and insists that it is time to get up and move around. Usually patients will get upset, because they think it is much too soon to be getting up. But the nurse knows that in order for your body to heal quickly, you must get up and going so that your physical strength won't deteriorate.

So many believers have been in the first stage of recovery for far too long. Atrophy has set in, and their spiritual, emotional, and mental muscle tone is damaged. God will use all kinds of situations and people to "get you up." Don't get mad. You need to respond if you are going to experience healing.

Finally, once the healing has been completed, there will be a scar. My wife, Debbie, often tells people that every time they look at a scar they can either remember the hurt, or they can remember the healing. As she has said many times, "If you chose to look at the scar and remember God's healing, you will be a trophy of God's grace."

Let God Satisfy Your Needs

If we look again at Psalm 23, it says "You prepare a table before me in the presence of my enemies; You have anointed my head with oil; *my cup overflows*." As David concludes this verse, "my cup overflows" speaks of his total and complete satisfaction.

One of the main reasons we get hurt is because we look to people to meet needs in our lives that only God can fulfill. We want our wife or husband, child, parent, friend, employer, or pastor to satisfy us in a way that only God is capable of doing. Someone once said that everyone has a God-shaped hole in their heart—but so many of us spend our lives trying to fill that hole with other people or things. It just never works.

No person can give you absolute security. No person can give you total unconditional love. No person can satisfy all your needs perfectly all the time. God did not create you to have all your needs met by a human. You are going to spend your life in disappointment and frustration if you expect any person to make you fully happy and satisfied.

On the other hand, God is more than able to meet your needs. That is what David is saying when he states that, "my cup overflows." God continuously meets the greatest needs of life:

> **Hope:** "Now may the God of hope fill you with all joy and peace in believing, so that you will abound in hope by the power of the Holy Spirit," (Romans 15:13).
>
> **Love:** "And may the Lord cause you to increase and abound in love for one another, and for all people, just as we also do for you," (1 Thessalonians 3:12).
>
> **Joy:** "Until now you have asked for nothing in My name; ask and you will receive, so that your joy may be made full," (John 16:24).

The nomadic Bedouin people of the Middle East are excellent hosts and well known for making their guests feel welcome. A common custom when someone would come to call was to put a cup before them, which the host would fill with water. If the guest drank from the cup, they would immediately refill it. They would continually do this to ensure that the guest had more than enough. However, if someone took a drink and their host didn't refill it, it meant that they were ready for the guest to leave. It was a polite but unspoken way of indicating that the time had come for the visit to end.

Now there was also another custom to fill the cup until it flowed over and spilled upon the ground. If the host did that, he was saying, "Everything I have is yours. I will meet your needs to the best of my ability with everything that I have." In the same way, when you come and sit down at God's table, whatever your hurts, however deep your wounds, He will fill your cup to overflowing. He will meet all of your needs according to His riches in glory.

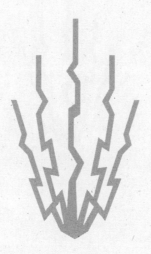

Chapter 7

SECURITY, CERTAINTY,
AND NO MORE FEAR

Surely goodness and loving-kindness will follow me all the days of my life, and I will dwell in the house of the Lord forever.
—Psalm 23:6

Dr. Maxwell Maltz was a well-known plastic surgeon and a pioneer in the field of self-help during the twentieth century. He authored several books, including *New Faces, New Futures*, in which he talked about his belief that physical deformities often have a profound effect on a person's emotional state. Dr. Maltz found that external imperfections—whether significant or relatively minor—were directly connected to his patients' internal sense of self-esteem, self-confidence, and self-worth. In other words, what his patients saw in the mirror defined how they viewed themselves as individuals.

Because of this correlation, Dr. Maltz was certain that fixing the physical problems would naturally change the underlying self-esteem issues. But after countless surgeries, he was surprised to discover that even after patients had their deformities corrected, they still had the same deep-seated insecurities. They continued to struggle with fear and rejection. Even though their outward appearance had changed, there was still something on the inside that caused them to doubt and fear.

"I changed how they looked completely, thinking that it was going to bring some self-confidence, some self-esteem, some self-worth; it would drive away their insecurity," Dr. Maltz said. "I discovered that no matter how much I changed their external appearance, it did not change the fear, the insecurity, the lack of self-esteem in their lives."

Dr. Maltz concluded that we must have an accurate and positive view of ourselves; otherwise we will get stuck in a continuing pattern of unhealthy behavior. He believed that if our self-image is flawed, all of our efforts in life will end in failure. It is not enough to change the outside man—the inside must change as well.

Our culture is fixated on appearances. We spend so much of our time dressing up, firming up, and living it up, thinking that will bring us fulfillment, security, and satisfaction, but it never does. Underneath all the external trimmings, we still wonder if we really matter; if anyone can love us for who we really are.

Most of us have experienced rejection of some kind that has bred insecurity and fear. Have you lost a job and that experience has left you with the constant worry that it might happen again? Perhaps you have been through a divorce, and you are unwilling to take a risk and experience that kind of rejection again. Or, perhaps you have been betrayed by a close friend or family member and you are afraid to trust anyone else. Ultimately there is only one solution to these fears. The only one who can bring healing is Jesus Christ.

His Goodness Pursues You

We have been studying the wisdom and truth found in arguably one of the most beloved passages of scripture—Psalm 23. In the final verse, David addresses the fundamental need that we all have for acceptance and security: "Surely goodness and loving-kindness will follow me all the days of my life, and I will dwell in the house of the LORD forever," (Psalm 23:6).

Here he is speaking of the ultimate security for those who are insecure. And if there ever was a man who needed safety and security, it was David. During his youth he was hated, persecuted, and at times even hunted by Saul, the King of Israel. Then later in his life, David was targeted again by his own son Absalom and the entire nation of Israel. Yet even in the midst of turmoil and betrayal, David always found refuge in the Lord.

The very first word in this verse, "Surely," is the word *ak* in the original Hebrew. A tiny but strong word, *ak* means "indeed; certain; without a doubt." David uses this emphatic term because he wants to convey his absolute certainty and confidence. He is utterly convinced that the Lord will take care of him.

Another important word to look at in this scripture is "follow." In English, this term is so anemic and passive. But within the context of this scripture, "follow" is a powerful word that speaks of an animal tracking down its prey.

Did you know that the cheetah is the fastest animal on land and can run up to 70 miles per hour? It is twice as fast as a greyhound or a horse. But what is really interesting about the cheetah is that when it chases its prey, it will fixate its attention on the prey's neck and will not move its eyes off of it. Nothing distracts a cheetah's focus once it commits to the pursuit.

That is what David is saying here. Just like a cheetah commits and races after its prey, *without a doubt* God's goodness—that which is best for our lives—pursues us. The Bible is full of testimony to the goodness of God: "The Lord is good to all, and His mercies are over all His works," (Psalm 145:9). God cares about every detail of your life. He wants the very best for you and so His goodness is constantly right at your heels—stalking you, pursuing you, chasing after you.

The apostle Paul also talks about God's involvement in our lives: "And we know that God causes all things to work together for good to those who love God, to those who are called according to His purpose," (Romans 8:28). It's important that we understand what this really means. This passage does not say that God is responsible for everything that happens. He is not the source of calamity, hardship, or suffering. The truth is that bad things happen to good people, and bad things happen to God's people. Nowhere in scripture will we find that believers are exempt from the hardships and struggles of life.

But what we do find is that even in the bad situations in life, God's goodness pursues His people. And no matter how bad our circumstances may be God will ultimately bring good out of them. That never changes. We change our minds but God does not. Our moods shift, but God's does not. Our devotion wanes, but God's devotion never falters. We have the ultimate security in knowing that one thing will never change: God is good.

His Mercy Works In You

David said along with God's goodness, His loving-kindness—or mercy—pursues us as well. Now goodness is what happens *to* us, mercy is what happens *in* us. Just as we are pursued by God's best, we are also pursued by God's blessing.

Here David uses the Hebrew word *hessed*, which we interpret as loving-kindness. The word is considered a covenant word because God used it when He made His covenant with Abraham and also with Moses and the children of Israel. The root of the word means "to bend over; to lean down."

Have you ever watched a mother care for her baby? Little ones need to be held and cuddled, comforted and soothed. She will continually bend over and reach down in order to care for his needs, love him, and bless him. That is the same picture of the loving kindness of God who never grows tired of bending down to bless and care for us.

Personally I am glad that David says that we are pursued by loving-kindness and not by justice. I don't want justice—I want

God's mercy. Psalm 103 speaks of how God cares for His people:

> Bless the Lord, O my soul, and all that is
> within me, bless His holy name.
> Bless the Lord, O my soul, and forget
> none of His benefits;
> Who pardons all your iniquities, who
> heals all your diseases;
> Who redeems your life from the pit, Who
> crowns you with loving-kindness and
> compassion;
> Who satisfies your years with good
> things, So that your youth is renewed
> like the eagle.
> The Lord performs righteous deeds and
> judgments for all who are oppressed.
> He made known His ways to Moses, His
> acts to the sons of Israel.
> The Lord is compassionate and gracious,
> slow to anger and abounding in loving-
> kindness.
> He will not always strive with us, nor will
> He keep His anger forever.
> He has not dealt with us according to
> our sins, nor rewarded us according to
> our iniquities.
> For as high as the heavens are above the
> earth, so great is His loving-kindness

toward those who fear Him.
—Psalm 103:1-11

The loving-kindness of God follows us all the days of our lives. It pursues us and stalks us relentlessly. It is limitless and He gives it freely.

We all will experience difficult days. Some will be days of sickness, others days of frustration, and even occasional days where we struggle with insecurity and fear. But we will never experience a single day apart from God's goodness and mercy. God's goodness watches over us, and His mercy works in us regardless of what kind of day we are having. Here are four distinct characteristics of God's goodness and His mercy:

God's Goodness

1. Provides and Protects
2. Supplies
3. Helps
4. Gives what we don't deserve

God's Mercy

1. Pardons and Forgives
2. Soothes
3. Heals
4. Holds back what we do deserve

For those of us who know the Lord as their Shepherd, He is not only watching over us in His goodness, but He is also working in us with His loving-kindness. That is completely different from what pursues the wicked and the ungodly. The Bible says, "Let their way be dark and slippery, with the angel of the Lord pursuing them on," (Psalm 35:6). Rest assured, the nature of that pursuit is completely different!

Several years ago, my wife and I went to the Highland Games at Grandfather Mountain where all of the Scottish clans come together to celebrate and compete. One of the things I witnessed first-hand was how the magnificent border collies move the sheep. The farmer sends the dogs out to bring the sheep in at night and they go and stay on the heels of the sheep until they are all safely in the fold.

It is really something to see these dogs work. They move back and forth carefully, always watching the sheep and monitoring where the flock is moving. Constantly in motion, they circle back and forth, never hurting or harassing the sheep, but steering them in the direction the shepherd wants to go. That is exactly what God's goodness and mercy do—they relentlessly stay on our heels until we are home.

Heaven Waits Before You

We've looked at the first part of this final verse, but there is more. "Surely goodness and loving-kindness will follow me all the days of my life, *and I will dwell in the house of the Lord forever*," (Psalm 23:6).

Notice the conjunction here. That little word "and" is so important—it ties together yesterday, today, and all of our tomorrows. God's plan for our lives is for His goodness and mercy to pursue us all the days of our lives here on this earth. But that is not the end. There is so much more.

Throughout this Psalm, we have followed David as he has traveled along the Shepherd's path through the green pastures and quiet waters of the lowlands, up through the valley of the shadow of death, and into the highlands. Now he is headed home.

When David speaks of dwelling in the house of the Lord, he is not referring to the temple; he is speaking of the Father's house in heaven. What awaits us at the Father's house?

Reward. We are told that there are rewards already prepared for us at the Father's house.

Reunion. We will be reunited with our loved ones who have gone before us in the Lord.

Reassignment. God gave man work in the garden, even before the fall of Adam and Eve. When man rebelled against God, work became laborious, tiresome, and frustrating. When we reach the Father's house there will be work, but it will be like nothing we have experienced before. We will have a perfect creativity, a perfect ability, and a perfect environment that our minds cannot even conceive of here.

Release. We will be released from every burden and failing of this world: sin, suffering, sickness, sorrow, fear, despair, depression, pain, and more.

Have you shouldered a burden that you simply could not bear? Have you lost a life-long mate? Have you been robbed of your dream? Do you suffer from a physical or emotional illness that will not be healed in this life? Are you in a relationship that is unfulfilling? Do you have an ongoing struggle to manage the most basic needs for your family? Do you face challenges that outweigh your ability to hold up?

Then David is speaking to you. You are tired. It is hard for you to see the Celestial City through the storm. You wonder how you will ever make it through. But David says if you know the Lord as your Shepherd, all of glory waits before you.

God never said the journey would be easy, but He did say that the destination would be worthwhile. He may not do what you want, but He can be counted on to do what is best and what is right. He is the Father of forward motion. Trust Him, He will get you home. The trials and tribulations of the journey will be forgotten in the joys of the feast.

The Lord is my Shepherd. He is beneath me in the green pastures. He is beside me in the still waters. He is with me in the valley of the shadow of death. He is around me in the presence of my enemies. He is above me, anointing my head with oil. He is near me, guiding me into the right paths. He is behind me. His goodness and loving-kindness pursue me. And He is before me in heaven, where I will dwell in His house forever. Now that is Hope!

STUDY GUIDE
AND NOTES

Study Guide

Chapter 1
WORRY – THE FAMILIAR FACE OF FEAR

1. Sherlock Holmes made the famous observation to his good friend Dr. Watson, "You have not observed. And yet you have seen." What situations have occurred in your life where you "saw" but did not really "observe"? Was there evidence that God was trying to show you something? If so, what was it? If you knew then what you know now, what would you have done differently?

2. Worry is just one of the many faces of fear. Do you struggle with worry? In what other ways does fear manifest itself in your life?

3. Psalm 23 presents an analogy comparing God to a shepherd. How does David's personal experience as a shepherd affect how you read and interpret Psalm 23? What pictures come to mind about a shepherd caring for his sheep? How do these images help you understand more about God and how He cares for you?

4. We know that worry is unhelpful, unreasonable, unhealthy, and unnatural. What are some examples from your own life where this has proven to be true?

NOTES

Study Guide

Chapter 2
RESTLESSNESS

1. Have you ever allowed fear to sabotage your goals or undermine your dreams? If so, what happened? What could you have done differently?

2. "Secular Spiritualists" are people who claim to have faith in God, yet live like the rest of secular society. How does your lifestyle testify to your faith? In what ways do you struggle with secular influences?

3. Webster's dictionary defines "restless" as: *lacking or denying rest: uneasy; continuously moving: unquiet; characterized by or manifesting unrest especially of mind; also: changeful, discontented.* Have you ever felt this way? What were the circumstances that caused you to experience restlessness? How does surrendering control of your life to the Lord help alleviate these "symptoms"?

4. If God is the Shepherd, we are His sheep. What characteristics do we share with sheep? How does this affect the way we relate to God?

NOTES

Study Guide

Chapter 3
THE FEAR OF NO RETURN

1. What part of Robert Robinson's story impacted you the most? How is it possible for someone to be sincerely saved by grace and so gifted by God, yet struggle so mightily with his own faith? If the words of Robinson's hymn truthfully reflect his convictions and faith at the time he wrote them, what do you think was the most significant thing that changed in his life?

2. We all have mistakes that we regret in our past. What choices do you regret in your own life? Have you ever felt that your sin was so great you could not turn to God for help? Is this a legitimate or rational fear? In what ways do unforgiveness, guilt, and grief steal from us?

3. Jesus said, "Judge not, and you shall not be judged; condemn not, and you shall not be condemned; forgive, and you shall be forgiven," (Luke 6:37 kjv). Why is it important to forgive? Do you struggle with forgiving people that have hurt you? Why is forgiveness necessary if we want to receive God's restoration? What consequences do we face if we carry grudges and do not forgive?

NOTES

Study Guide

Chapter 4
AIMLESSNESS

1. The tragedy of Tiananmen Square crushed the hopes of countless Chinese people, and in the emotional fall-out, thousands of young students committed suicide. But if the revolt had been successful, would democracy truly have fulfilled all their dreams and expectations? What purpose might God have had in allowing it to fail? How was the democracy movement in China similar to the current political climate in America today? Is "change" really the answer? Why or why not?

2. Aimlessness is the lack of direction, purpose, and hope. In what ways is aimlessness contrary to God's nature? Have there been times in your life where you have felt adrift or hopeless about the future? What caused you to feel that way?

3. The Bible says, "'For I know the plans that I have for you,' declares the Lord, 'plans for welfare and not for calamity to give you a future and a hope,'" (Jeremiah 29:11). How does this promise help us overcome fear and aimlessness? Why is it so important that we allow the Lord to guide us?

4. We know that the Lord guides us through the Word of God, the leading of the Holy Spirit, wise Godly counsel, and even through our own personalities. What are some examples of how God has used each of these in your own life? What lessons have you learned through those experiences?

NOTES

Study Guide

Chapter 5
THROUGH THE VALLEYS

1. Psalm 23:4 may very well be the most familiar verse in the Bible: "*Even though I walk through the valley of the shadow of death, I fear no evil, for You are with me; Your rod and Your staff, they comfort me.*" How is David able to not fear, even in the shadow of death? Why is it important to remember that God takes us **through** the valley... not just **into** it?

2. The valleys in Israel are named for the challenges, conflicts, and defeats of the Jewish people, such as: trouble, giants, weeping, slaughter, judgment, decision. List some of the valleys that you have faced in your own life. How did God bring you through them? In what ways does God use valleys in our lives to bless us?

3. We've learned that the valleys in Israel can be dark, depressing, and difficult to travel. How does this mirror the reality of life? Is it realistic for Christians to expect an easy, pleasant path once they receive Jesus? What does the Bible have to say about this? Why do you think so many Christians are unprepared for the struggles that lie ahead?

4. Jesus said, "I have come as Light into the world, so that everyone who believes in Me will not remain in darkness," (John 12:46). What does this scripture mean to you? If you know Jesus, how has your life changed since you found the Light?

5. Within the context of the illustration that shadows are created when light meets darkness, we know that the best way to overcome fear in the valley is to face the Light. But Jesus also said about those believers who follow Him, "You are the light of the world. A city set on a hill cannot be hidden," (Matthew 5:14). From a practical perspective, how can we bring His light to others who are facing dark times?

NOTES

Study Guide

Chapter 6
GOD'S RESPONSE TO OUR HURT

1. We know that all of us get hurt at one time or another. What relationships or situations have caused pain in your life? How did you handle them? In what ways does God also use relationships to help bring healing?

2. God ministers to us and brings healing in our lives through fellowship, worship, prayer, and ministry. Is any one of these elements more important than the others? Why does God require us to "do something" in order to receive healing?

3. Just because God has healed us does not mean we do not bear scars. What do you think about when you look at your own scars? Do they seem ugly or beautiful? Are they a source of bitterness and anger, or joy and peace? How might our scars actually be a blessing in the lives of others?

NOTES

Study Guide

Chapter 7
SECURITY, CERTAINTY, AND NO MORE FEAR

1. Dr. Maltz learned that changing a person's outward appearance had virtually no effect on their inward insecurities and fears. How is this demonstrated by today's celebrity culture? What insecurities and fears do you struggle with? How do they contrast with what God says about who you are?

2. How does it make you feel to know that God's goodness pursues you in the same way an animal hunts its prey? Do you really expect to receive His goodness, or are you accustomed to expecting the worst? What is the difference between God's goodness and His mercy?

3. Does it bring you comfort to think about what God has waiting for you at the end of your journey? In what ways does real hope change our lives now—not just for eternity?

NOTES

About the Author

Dr. Mac Brunson is the Senior Pastor of First Baptist Church in Jacksonville, Florida. He holds degrees from Furman University and Southwestern Seminary. Dr. Brunson pastored in South Carolina, Virginia, North Carolina, and Texas before going to Jacksonville in 2006.

A well-known speaker and experienced minister, Dr. Brunson was appointed president of the Southern Baptist Convention Pastor's Conference in 2003. He is heard on numerous radio and television stations around the world weekly.

Dr. Brunson and his wife, Debbie, are the parents of three grown children—Courtney, Trey, and Wills—and have two grandchildren. As a family committed to missions, the Brunsons have taken trips together to Argentina, England, Lebanon, Russia, and to Ukraine.